D0208339

The
ANONYMOUS PRESS
MINI EDITION
of
ALCOHOLICS
ANONYMOUS

STATEMENT OF PURPOSE

The Anonymous Press is made up of a bunch of A.A. members staying sober by carrying the message of A.A.. Our primary purpose is to carry the message of A.A. by making our basic text affordable to all. Were we can, we also try to make the text easier to study and understand.

We realize that A.A., The Fellowship that saved our lives, is held together by The Traditions so The Traditions are what guide us. All of our books are sold at cost. We have no employees and we are certainly not organized. Wherever possible our work is carried out by members of A.A. as service work.

Our efforts have resulted in the distribution of our fellowship's basic text to tens of thousands of fellow alcoholics who otherwise may not have had a book of their own. Detoxes, rehabs, prisons and shelters can now afford to give away our text - offering countless alcoholics a chance to learn the unadulterated message of our program.

If you are a member of A.A. and would like to lend a hand to help in our work, volunteers and contributions are always welcome.

The Anonymous Press

The Anonymous Press
PO Box 1212, Malo WA 99150-1212 USA

USA	(800) 800-4398	FAX USA	(914) 962-1395
United Kingdom	0800-96-2375	Eire	1800-55-7896
Australia	1-800-122-685	E-mail:	anonpress@cyberholic.com

First Printing 1992   Eighth Printing 1997

The contents of this book can be found on the Internet at:
http://www.recovery.org/aa

This site is not run by The Anonymous Press,
but we contribute to it as a service to our fellows.

The gray areas do not appear in the original text.
Library of Congress Catalog No. 93-079125
ISBN 0-9637666-0-0
Printed in the United States of America

FOREWORD

WE, OF Alcoholics Anonymous, are more than one hundred men and women who have recovered from a seemingly hopeless state of mind and body. To show other alcoholics *precisely how we have recovered* is the main purpose of this book. For them, we hope these pages will prove so convincing that no further authentication will be necessary. We think this account of our experiences will help everyone to better understand the alcoholic. Many do not comprehend that the alcoholic is a very sick person. And besides, we are sure that our way of living has its advantages for all.

It is important that we remain anonymous because we are too few, at present to handle the overwhelming number of personal appeals which may result from this publication. Being mostly business or professional folk, we could not well carry on our occupations in such an event. We would like it understood that our alcoholic work is an avocation.

When writing or speaking publicly about alcoholism, we urge each of our Fellowship to omit his personal name, designating himself instead as "a member of Alcoholics Anonymous."

Very earnestly we ask the press also, to observe this request, for otherwise we shall be greatly handicapped.

We are not an organization in the conventional

sense of the word. There are no fees or dues what-soever. The only requirement for membership is an honest desire to stop drinking. We are not allied with any particular faith, sect or denomination, nor do we oppose anyone. We simply wish to be helpful to those who are afflicted.

We shall be interested to hear from those who are getting results from this book, particularly from those who have commenced work with other alcoholics. We should like to be helpful to such cases.

Inquiry by scientific, medical, and religious societies will be welcomed.

ALCOHOLICS ANONYMOUS.

THE DOCTOR'S OPINION

*W*E OF Alcoholics Anonymous believe that the reader will be interested in the medical estimate of the plan of recovery described in this book. Convincing testimony must surely come from medical men who have had experience with the sufferings of our members and have witnessed our return to health. A well-known doctor, chief physician at a nationally prominent hospital specializing in alcoholic and drug addiction, gave Alcoholics Anonymous this letter:

To Whom It May Concern:

I have specialized in the treatment of alcoholism for many years.

In late 1934 I attended a patient who, though he had been a competent businessman of good earning capacity, was an alcoholic of a type I had come to regard as hopeless.

In the course of his third treatment he acquired certain ideas concerning a possible means of recovery. As part of his rehabilitation he commenced to present his conceptions to other alcoholics, impressing upon them that they must do likewise with still others. This has become the basis of a rapidly growing fellowship of these men and their families. This man and over one hundred others appear to have recovered.

I personally know scores of cases who were of the type with whom other methods had failed completely.

These facts appear to be of extreme medical importance; because of the extraordinary possibilities of rapid growth inherent in this group they may mark a new epoch in the annals of alcoholism. These men may well have a remedy for thousands of such situations.

You may rely absolutely on anything they say about themselves.

Very truly yours,
William D. Silkworth, M.D.

The physician who, at our request, gave us this letter, has been kind enough to enlarge upon his views in another statement which follows. In this statement he confirms what we who have suffered alcoholic torture must believe—that the body of the alcoholic is quite as abnormal as his mind. It did not satisfy us to be told that we could not control our drinking just because we were maladjusted to life, that we were in full flight from reality, or were outright mental defectives. These things were true to some extent, in fact, to a considerable extent with some of us. But we are sure that our bodies were sickened as well. In our belief, any picture of the alcoholic which leaves out this physical factor is incomplete.

The doctor's theory that we have an allergy to alcohol interests us. As laymen, our opinion as to its soundness may, of course, mean little. But as ex-problem drinkers, we can say that his explanation makes good sense. It explains many things for which we cannot otherwise account.

Though we work out our solution on the spiritual as well as an altruistic plane, we favor hospitalization for the alcoholic who is very jittery or befogged. More often than not, it is imperative that a man's brain be cleared before he is approached, as he has then a better chance of understanding and accepting what we have to offer.

The doctor writes:

The subject presented in this book seems to me to be of paramount importance to those afflicted with alcoholic addiction.

I say this after many years' experience as Medical Director of one of the oldest hospitals in the country treating alcoholic and drug addiction.

There was, therefore, a sense of real satisfaction when I was asked to contribute a few words on a subject which is covered in such masterly detail in these pages.

We doctors have realized for a long time that some form of moral psychology was of urgent importance to alcoholics, but its application presented difficulties beyond our conception. What with our ultra-modern standards, our scientific approach to everything, we are perhaps not well equipped to apply the powers of good that lie outside our synthetic knowledge.

Many years ago one of the leading contributors to this book came under our care in this hospital and while here he acquired some ideas which he put into practical application at once.

Later, he requested the privilege of being allowed to tell his story to other patients here and with some misgiving, we consented. The cases we have followed through have been most interesting; in fact, many of them are amazing. The unselfishness of these men as we have come to know them, the entire absence of profit motive, and their community spirit, is indeed inspiring to one who has labored long and wearily in this alcoholic field. They believe in themselves, and still more in the Power which pulls chronic alcoholics back from the gates of death.

Of course an alcoholic ought to be freed from his physical

craving for liquor, and this often requires a definite hospital procedure, before psychological measures can be of maximum benefit.

We believe, and so suggested a few years ago, that the action of alcohol on these chronic alcoholics is a manifestation of an allergy; that the phenomenon of craving is limited to this class and never occurs in the average temperate drinker. These allergic types can never safely use alcohol in any form at all; and once having formed the habit and found they cannot break it, once having lost their self-confidence, their reliance upon things human, their problems pile up on them and become astonishingly difficult to solve.

Frothy emotional appeal seldom suffices. The message which can interest and hold these alcoholic people must have depth and weight. In nearly all cases, their ideals must be grounded in a power greater than themselves, if they are to re-create their lives.

If any feel that as psychiatrists directing a hospital for alcoholics we appear somewhat sentimental, let them stand with us a while on the firing line, see the tragedies, the despairing wives, the little children; let the solving of these problems become a part of their daily work, and even of their sleeping moments, and the most cynical will not wonder that we have accepted and encouraged this movement. We feel, after many years of experience, that we have found nothing which has contributed more to the rehabilitation of these men than the altruistic movement now growing up among them.

Men and women drink essentially because they like the effect produced by alcohol. The sensation is so elusive that, while they admit it is injurious, they cannot after a time differentiate the true from the false. To them, their alcoholic life seems the only normal one. They are restless, irritable and discontented, unless they can again experience

the sense of ease and comfort which comes at once by taking a few drinks—drinks which they see others taking with
impunity. After they have succumbed to the desire again,
as so many do, and the phenomenon of craving develops,
they pass through the well-known stages of a spree, emerg-
ing remorseful, with a firm resolution not to drink again.
This is repeated over and over, and unless this person can
experience an entire psychic change there is very little hope
of his recovery.

On the other hand—and strange as this may seem to those
who do not understand—once a psychic change has occurred, the very same person who seemed doomed, who
had so many problems he despaired of ever solving them,
suddenly finds himself easily able to control his desire for
alcohol, the only effort necessary being that required to
follow a few simple rules.

Men have cried out to me in sincere and despairing appeal: "Doctor, I cannot go on like this! I have everything
to live for! I must stop, but I cannot! You must help me!"

Faced with this problem, if a doctor is honest with himself, he must sometimes feel his own inadequacy. Although
he gives all that is in him, it often is not enough. One feels
that something more than human power is needed to produce the essential psychic change. Though the aggregate
of recoveries resulting from psychiatric effort is considerable, we physicians must admit we have made little impression upon the problem as a whole. Many types do not
respond to the ordinary psychological approach.

I do not hold with those who believe that alcoholism is
entirely a problem of mental control. I have had many
men who had, for example, worked a period of months on
some problem or business deal which was to be settled on
a certain date, favorably to them. They took a drink a day
or so prior to the date, and then the phenomenon of craving
at once became paramount to all other interests so that the

important appointment was not met. These men were not drinking to escape; they were drinking to overcome a craving beyond their mental control.

There are many situations which arise out of the phenomenon of craving which cause men to make the supreme sacrifice rather than continue to fight.

The classification of alcoholics seems most difficult, and in much detail is outside the scope of this book. There are, of course, the psychopaths who are emotionally unstable. We are all familiar with this type. They are always "going on the wagon for keeps." They are over-remorseful and make many resolutions, but never a decision.

There is the type of man who is unwilling to admit that he cannot take a drink. He plans various ways of drinking. He changes his brand or his environment. There is the type who always believes that after being entirely free from alcohol for a period of time he can take a drink without danger. There is the manic-depressive type, who is, perhaps, the least understood by his friends, and about whom a whole chapter could be written.

Then there are types entirely normal in every respect except in the effect alcohol has upon them. They are often able, intelligent, friendly people.

All these, and many others, have one symptom in common: they cannot start drinking without developing the phenomenon of craving. This phenomenon, as we have suggested, may be the manifestation of an allergy which differentiates these people, and sets them apart as a distinct entity. It has never been, by any treatment with which we are familiar, permanently eradicated. The only relief we have to suggest is entire abstinence.

This immediately precipitates us into a seething caldron of debate. Much has been written pro and con, but among physicians, the general opinion seems to be that most chronic alcoholics are doomed.

What is the solution? Perhaps I can best answer this by relating one of my experiences.

About one year prior to this experience a man was brought in to be treated for chronic alcoholism. He had but partially recovered from a gastric hemorrhage and seemed to be a case of pathological mental deterioration. He had lost everything worthwhile in life and was only living, one might say, to drink. He frankly admitted and believed that for him there was no hope. Following the elimination of alcohol, there was found to be no permanent brain injury. He accepted the plan outlined in this book. One year later he called to see me, and I experienced a very strange sensation. I knew the man by name, and partly recognized his features, but there all resemblance ended. From a trembling, despairing, nervous wreck, had emerged a man brimming over with self-reliance and contentment. I talked with him for some time, but was not able to bring myself to feel that I had known him before. To me he was a stranger, and so he left me. A long time has passed with no return to alcohol.

When I need a mental uplift, I often think of another case brought in by a physician prominent in New York. The patient had made his own diagnosis, and deciding his situation hopeless, had hidden in a deserted barn determined to die. He was rescued by a searching party, and, in desperate condition, brought to me. Following his physical rehabilitation, he had a talk with me in which he frankly stated he thought the treatment a waste of effort, unless I could assure him, which no one ever had, that in the future he would have the "will power" to resist the impulse to drink.

His alcoholic problem was so complex, and his depression so great, that we felt his only hope would be through what we then called "moral psychology," and we doubted if even that would have any effect.

However, he did become "sold" on the ideas contained in this book. He has not had a drink for a great many years. I see him now and then and he is as fine a specimen of manhood as one could wish to meet.

I earnestly advise every alcoholic to read this book through, and though perhaps he came to scoff, he may remain to pray.

William D. Silkworth, M.D.

Chapter 1

BILL'S STORY

*W*AR FEVER ran high in the New England town to which we new, young officers from Plattsburg were assigned, and we were flattered when the first citizens took us to their homes, making us feel heroic. Here was love, applause, war; moments sublime with intervals hilarious. I was part of life at last, and in the midst of the excitement I discovered liquor. I forgot the strong warnings and the prejudices of my people concerning drink. In time we sailed for "Over There." I was very lonely and again turned to alcohol.

We landed in England. I visited Winchester Cathedral. Much moved, I wandered outside. My attention was caught by a doggerel on an old tombstone:

> "Here lies a Hampshire Grenadier
> Who caught his death
> Drinking cold small beer.
> A good soldier is ne'er forgot
> Whether he dieth by musket
> Or by pot."

Ominous warning—which I failed to heed.

Twenty-two, and a veteran of foreign wars, I went home at last. I fancied myself a leader, for had not the men of my battery given me a special token of appreciation? My talent for leadership, I imagined, would place me at the head of vast enterprises which I would manage with the utmost assurance.

I took a night law course, and obtained employment as investigator for a surety company. The drive for success was on. I'd prove to the world I was important. My work took me about Wall Street and little by little I became interested in the market. Many people lost money—but some became very rich. Why not I? I studied economics and business as well as law. Potential alcoholic that I was, I nearly failed my law course. At one of the finals I was too drunk to think or write. Though my drinking was not yet continuous, it disturbed my wife. We had long talks when I would still her forebodings by telling her that men of genius conceived their best projects when drunk; that the most majestic constructions of philosophic thought were so derived.

By the time I had completed the course, I knew the law was not for me. The inviting maelstrom of Wall Street had me in its grip. Business and financial leaders were my heroes. Out of this alloy of drink and speculation, I commenced to forge the weapon that one day would turn in its flight like a boomerang and all but cut me to ribbons. Living modestly, my wife and I saved $1,000. It went into certain securities, then cheap and rather unpopular. I rightly imagined that they would some day have a great rise. I failed to persuade my broker friends to send me out looking over factories and managements, but my wife and I decided to go anyway. I had developed a theory that most people lost money in stocks through ignorance of markets. I discovered many more reasons later on.

We gave up our positions and off we roared on a motorcycle, the sidecar stuffed with tent, blankets, a change of clothes, and three huge volumes of a financial reference service. Our friends thought a lunacy commission should be appointed. Perhaps they were right. I had had some success at speculation, so we had a little money, but we once worked on a farm for a month to avoid drawing on our small capital. That was the last honest manual labor on my part for many a day. We covered the whole eastern United States in a year. At the end of it, my reports to Wall Street procured me a position there and the use of a large expense account. The exercise of an option brought in more money, leaving us with a profit of several thousand dollars for that year.

For the next few years fortune threw money and applause my way. I had arrived. My judgment and ideas were followed by many to the tune of paper millions. The great boom of the late twenties was seething and swelling. Drink was taking an important and exhilarating part in my life. There was loud talk in the jazz places uptown. Everyone spent in thousands and chattered in millions. Scoffers could scoff and be damned. I made a host of fair-weather friends.

My drinking assumed more serious proportions, continuing all day and almost every night. The remonstrances of my friends terminated in a row and I became a lone wolf. There were many unhappy scenes in our sumptuous apartment. There had been no real infidelity, for loyalty to my wife, helped at times by extreme drunkenness, kept me out of those scrapes.

In 1929 I contracted golf fever. We went at once to the country, my wife to applaud while I started out to overtake Walter Hagen.[1] Liquor caught up with me much faster than I came up behind Walter. I began to be jittery in the morning. Golf permitted drinking every day and every night. It was fun to carom around the exclusive course which had inspired such awe in me as a lad. I acquired the impeccable coat of tan one sees upon the well-to-do. The local banker watched me whirl fat checks in and out of his till with amused skepticism.

Abruptly in October 1929 hell broke loose on the New York stock exchange. After one of those days of inferno, I wobbled from a hotel bar to a brokerage office. It was eight o'clock—five hours after the market closed. The ticker still clattered. I was staring at an inch of the tape which bore the inscription XYZ-32. It had been 52 that morning. I was finished and so were many friends. The papers reported men jumping to death from the towers of High Finance. That disgusted me. I would not jump. I went back to the bar. My friends had dropped several million since ten o'clock—so what? Tomorrow was another day. As I drank, the old fierce determination to win came back.

Next morning I telephoned a friend in Montreal. He had plenty of money left and thought I had better go to Canada. By the following spring we were living in our accustomed style. I felt like Napoleon returning from Elba.[2,3] No St. Helena for me![4] But drinking caught up with me again and my generous friend had to let me go. This time we stayed broke.

We went to live with my wife's parents. I found a job; then lost it as the result of a brawl with a taxi driver. Mercifully, no one could guess that I was to have no real employment for five years, or hardly draw a sober breath. My wife began to work in a department store, coming home exhausted to find me drunk.

I became an unwelcome hanger-on at brokerage places.

Liquor ceased to be a luxury; it became a necessity. "Bathtub" gin, two bottles a day, and often three, got to be routine.[5] Sometimes a small deal would net a few hundred dollars, and I would pay my bills at the bars and delicatessens. This went on endlessly, and I began to waken very early in the morning shaking violently. A tumbler full of gin followed by half a dozen bottles of beer would be required if I were to eat any breakfast. Nevertheless, I still thought I could control the situation, and there were periods of sobriety which renewed my wife's hope.

Gradually things got worse. The house was taken over by the mortgage holder, my mother-in-law died, my wife and father-in-law became ill.

Then I got a promising business opportunity. Stocks were at the low point of 1932, and I had somehow formed a group to buy. I was to share generously in the profits. Then I went on a prodigious bender, and that chance vanished.

I woke up. This had to be stopped. I saw I could not take so much as one drink. I was through forever. Before then, I had written lots of sweet promises, but my wife happily observed that this time I meant business. And so I did.

Shortly afterward I came home drunk. There had been no fight. Where had been my high resolve? I simply didn't know. It hadn't even come to mind. Someone had pushed a drink my way, and I had taken it. Was I crazy? I began to wonder, for such an appalling lack of perspective seemed near being just that.

Renewing my resolve, I tried again. Some time

passed, and confidence began to be replaced by cock-sure-
ness. I could laugh at the gin mills. Now I had what it
takes! One day I walked into a cafe to telephone. In no
time I was beating on the bar asking myself how it happened. As the whisky rose to my head I told myself I would
manage better next time, but I might as well get good and
drunk then. And I did.

The remorse, horror and hopelessness of the next morning are unforgettable. The courage to do battle was not
there. My brain raced uncontrollably and there was a terrible sense of impending calamity. I hardly dared cross the
street, lest I collapse and be run down by an early morning
truck, for it was scarcely daylight. An all night place supplied me with a dozen glasses of ale. My writhing nerves
were stilled at last. A morning paper told me the market
had gone to hell again. Well, so had I. The market would
recover, but I wouldn't. That was a hard thought. Should
I kill myself? No—not now. Then a mental fog settled
down. Gin would fix that. So two bottles, and—oblivion.

The mind and body are marvelous mechanisms, for mine
endured this agony two more years. Sometimes I stole from
my wife's slender purse when the morning terror and mad-
ness were on me. Again I swayed dizzily before an open
window, or the medicine cabinet where there was poison,
cursing myself for a weakling. There were flights from
city to country and back, as my wife and I sought escape.
Then came the night when the physical and mental torture
was so hellish I feared I would burst through my window,
sash and all. Somehow I managed to drag my mattress to a
lower floor, lest I suddenly leap. A doctor came with

a heavy sedative. Next day found me drinking both gin and sedative. This combination soon landed me on the rocks. People feared for my sanity. So did I. I could eat little or nothing when drinking, and I was forty pounds under weight.

My brother-in-law is a physician, and through his kindness and that of my mother I was placed in a nationally-known hospital for the mental and physical rehabilitation of alcoholics. Under the so-called belladonna treatment my brain cleared.[6] Hydrotherapy and mild exercise helped much. Best of all, I met a kind doctor who explained that though certainly selfish and foolish, I had been seriously ill, bodily and mentally.

It relieved me somewhat to learn that in alcoholics the will is amazingly weakened when it comes to combating liquor, though it often remains strong in other respects. My incredible behavior in the face of a desperate desire to stop was explained. Understanding myself now, I fared forth in high hope. For three for four months the goose hung high. I went to town regularly and even made a little money. Surely this was the answer—self-knowledge.

But it was not, for the frightful day came when I drank once more. The curve of my declining moral and bodily health fell off like a ski-jump. After a time I returned to the hospital. This was the finish, the curtain, it seemed to me. My weary and despairing wife was informed that it would all end with heart failure during delirium tremens, or I would develop a wet brain, perhaps within a year. She would soon have to give me over to the undertaker or the asylum.

They did not need to tell me. I knew, and almost welcomed the idea. It was a devastating blow to my pride. I, who had thought so well of myself and my abilities, of my capacity to surmount obstacles, was cornered at last. Now I was to plunge into the dark, joining that endless procession of sots who had gone on before. I thought of my poor wife. There had been much happiness after all. What would I not give to make amends. But that was over now.

No words can tell of the loneliness and despair I found in that bitter morass of self-pity. Quicksand stretched around me in all directions. I had met my match. I had been overwhelmed. Alcohol was my master.

Trembling, I stepped from the hospital a broken man. Fear sobered me for a bit. Then came the insidious insanity of that first drink, and on Armistice Day 1934, I was off again.[7] Everyone became resigned to the certainty that I would have to be shut up somewhere, or would stumble along to a miserable end. How dark it is before the dawn! In reality that was the beginning of my last debauch. I was soon to be catapulted into what I like to call the fourth dimension of existence. I was to know happiness, peace, and usefulness, in a way of life that is incredibly more wonderful as time passes.

Near the end of that bleak November, I sat drinking in my kitchen. With a certain satisfaction I reflected there was enough gin concealed about the house to carry me through that night and the next day. My wife was at work. I wondered whether I dared hide a full bottle of gin near the head of our bed. I would need it before daylight.

My musing was interrupted by the telephone. The cheery voice of an old school friend asked if he might come over. *He was sober.* It was years since I could re-member his coming to New York in that condition. I was amazed. Rumor had it that he had been committed for alcoholic insanity. I wondered how he had escaped. Of course he would have dinner, and then I could drink openly with him. Unmindful of his welfare, I thought only of recapturing the spirit of other days. There was that time we had chartered an airplane to complete a jag! His com-ing was an oasis in this dreary desert of futility. The very thing—an oasis! Drinkers are like that.

The door opened and he stood there, fresh-skinned and glowing. There was something about his eyes. He was inexplicably different. What had happened?

I pushed a drink across the table. He refused it. Disap-pointed but curious, I wondered what had got into the fel-low. He wasn't himself.

"Come, what's this all about?" I queried.

He looked straight at me. Simply, but smilingly, he said, "I've got religion."

I was aghast. So that was it—last summer an alcoholic crackpot; now, I suspected, a little cracked about religion. He had that starry-eyed look. Yes, the old boy was on fire all right. But bless his heart, let him rant! Besides, my gin would last longer than his preaching.

But he did no ranting. In a matter of fact way he told how two men had appeared in court, persuading the judge to suspend his commitment. They had told of a simple religious idea and a practical program of action. That was two months ago and the result was self-evident. It worked!

He had come to pass his experience along to me—if

I cared to have it. I was shocked, but interested. Certainly I was interested. I had to be, for I was hopeless.

He talked for hours. Childhood memories rose before me. I could almost hear the sound of the preacher's voice as I sat, on still Sundays, way over there on the hillside; there was that proffered temperance pledge I never signed; my grandfather's good natured contempt of some church folk and their doings; his insistence that the spheres really had their music; but his denial of the preacher's right to tell him how he must listen; his fearlessness as he spoke of these things just before he died; these recollections welled up from the past. They made me swallow hard.

That war-time day in old Winchester Cathedral came back again.

I had always believed in a Power greater than myself. I had often pondered these things. I was not an atheist. Few people really are, for that means blind faith in the strange proposition that this universe originated in a cipher and aimlessly rushes nowhere. My intellectual heroes, the chemists, the astronomers, even the evolutionists, suggested vast laws and forces at work. Despite contrary indications, I had little doubt that a mighty purpose and rhythm underlay all. How could there be so much of precise and immutable law, and no intelligence? I simply had to believe in a Spirit of the Universe, who knew neither time nor limitation. But that was as far as I had gone.

With ministers, and the world's religions, I parted right there. When they talked of a God personal to me, who was love, superhuman strength and direction, I became irritated and my mind snapped shut against such a theory.

To Christ I conceded the certainty of a great man, not too closely followed by those who claimed Him. His moral teaching—most excellent. For myself, I had adopted those parts which seemed convenient and not too difficult; the rest I disregarded.

The wars which had been fought, the burnings and chicanery that religious dispute had facilitated, made me sick. I honestly doubted whether, on balance, the religions of mankind had done any good. Judging from what I had seen in Europe and since, the power of God in human affairs was negligible, the Brotherhood of Man a grim jest. If there was a Devil, he seemed the Boss Universal, and he certainly had me.

But my friend sat before me, and he made the point-blank declaration that God had done for him what he could not do for himself. His human will had failed. Doctors had pronounced him incurable. Society was about to lock him up. Like myself, he had admitted complete defeat. Then he had, in effect, been raised from the dead, suddenly taken from the scrap heap to a level of life better than the best he had ever known!

Had this power originated in him? Obviously it had not. There had been no more power in him than there was in me at the minute; and this was none at all.

That floored me. It began to look as though religious people were right after all. Here was something at work in a human heart which had done the impossible. My ideas about miracles were drastically revised right then. Never mind the musty past; here sat a miracle directly across the kitchen table. He shouted great tidings.

I saw that my friend was much more than inwardly

reorganized. He was on a different footing. His roots grasped a new soil.

Despite the living example of my friend there remained in me the vestiges of my old prejudice. The word God still aroused a certain antipathy. When the thought was expressed that there might be a God personal to me this feeling was intensified. I didn't like the idea. I could go for such conceptions as Creative Intelligence, Universal Mind or Spirit of Nature but I resisted the thought of a Czar of the Heavens, however loving His sway might be.[8] I have since talked with scores of men who felt the same way.

My friend suggested what then seemed a novel idea. He said, *"Why don't you choose your own conception of God?"*

That statement hit me hard. It melted the icy intellectual mountain in whose shadow I had lived and shivered many years. I stood in the sunlight at last.

It was only a matter of being willing to believe in a Power greater than myself. Nothing more was required of me to make my beginning. I saw that growth could start from that point. Upon a foundation of complete willingness I might build what I saw in my friend. Would I have it? Of course I would!

Thus was I convinced that God is concerned with us humans when we want Him enough. At long last I saw, I felt, I believed. Scales of pride and prejudice fell from my eyes. A new world came into view.

The real significance of my experience in the Cathedral burst upon me. For a brief moment, I had needed and wanted God. There had been a humble willingness to have Him with me—and He came. But soon the sense of His presence had been blotted out by worldly clamors, mostly those within myself. And so it had been ever since. How blind I had been.

At the hospital I was separated from alcohol for the last time. Treatment seemed wise, for I showed signs of delirium tremens.

There I humbly offered myself to God, as I then understood Him, to do with me as He would. I placed myself unreservedly under His care and direction. I admitted for the first time that of myself I was nothing; that without Him I was lost. I ruthlessly faced my sins and became willing to have my new-found Friend take them away, root and branch. I have not had a drink since.

My schoolmate visited me, and I fully acquainted him with my problems and deficiencies. We made a list of people I had hurt or toward whom I felt resentment. I expressed my entire willingness to approach these individuals, admitting my wrong. Never was I to be critical of them. I was to right all such matters to the utmost of my ability.

I was to test my thinking by the new God-consciousness within. Common sense would thus become uncommon sense. I was to sit quietly when in doubt, asking only for direction and strength to meet my problems as He would have me. Never was I to pray for myself, except as my requests bore on my usefulness to others. Then only might I expect to receive. But that would be in great measure.

My friend promised when these things were done I would enter upon a new relationship with my Creator; that I would have the elements of a way of living which answered all my problems. Belief in the power of God, plus enough willingness, honesty and humility to establish and maintain the new order of things, were the essential requirements.

Simple, but not easy; a price had to be paid. It meant destruction of self-centeredness. I must turn in all things to the Father of Light who presides over us all.

These were revolutionary and drastic proposals, but the moment I fully accepted them, the effect was electric. There was a sense of victory, followed by such a peace and serenity as I had never known. There was utter confidence. I felt lifted up, as though the great clean wind of a mountain top blew through and through. God comes to most men gradually, but His impact on me was sudden and profound.

For a moment I was alarmed, and called my friend, the doctor, to ask if I were still sane. He listened in wonder as I talked.

Finally he shook his head saying, "Something has happened to you I don't understand. But you had better hang on to it. Anything is better than the way you were." The good doctor now sees many men who have such experiences. He knows that they are real.

While I lay in the hospital the thought came that there were thousands of hopeless alcoholics who might be glad to have what had been so freely given me. Perhaps I could help some of them. They in turn might work with others.

My friend had emphasized the absolute necessity of demonstrating these principles in all my affairs. Particularly was it imperative to work with others as he had worked with me. Faith without works was dead, he said. And how appallingly true for the alcoholic! For if an alcoholic failed to perfect and enlarge his spiritual life through work and self-sacrifice for others, he could not survive the certain trials and low spots ahead. If he did not work, he would surely drink again, and if he drank, he would surely die. Then faith would be dead indeed. With us it is just like that.

My wife and I abandoned ourselves with enthusiasm to the idea of helping other alcoholics to a solution of their problems. It was fortunate, for my old business associates remained skeptical for a year and a half, during which I found little work. I was not too well at the time, and was plagued by waves of self-pity and resentment. This sometimes nearly drove me back to drink, but I soon found that when all other measures failed, work with another alcoholic would save the day. Many times I have gone to my old hospital in despair. On talking to a man there, I would be amazingly lifted up and set on my feet. It is a design for living that works in rough going.

We commenced to make many fast friends and a fellowship has grown up among us of which it is a wonderful thing to feel a part. The joy of living we really have, even under pressure and difficulty. I have seen hundreds of families set their feet in the path that really goes somewhere; have seen the most impossible domestic situations righted; feuds and bitterness of all sorts wiped out. I have seen men come out of asylums and resume a vital place in the lives of their families and communities. Business and professional men have regained their standing. There is scarcely any form of trouble and misery which has not been overcome among us. In one western city and its environs there are one thousand of us and our families. We meet frequently so that newcomers may find the fellowship they seek. At these informal gatherings one may often see from 50 to 200 persons. We are growing in numbers and power.

An alcoholic in his cups is an unlovely creature. Our struggles with them are variously strenuous, comic, and tragic. One poor chap committed suicide in my home. He could not, or would not, see our way of life.

There is, however a vast amount of fun about it all. I suppose some would be shocked at our seeming worldliness and levity. But just underneath there is deadly earnestness. Faith has to work twenty-four hours a day in and through us, or we perish.

Most of us feel we need look no further for Utopia. We have it with us right here and now. Each day my friend's simple talk in our kitchen multiplies itself in a widening circle of peace on earth and good will to men.

Note	Page	
1	3	Walter Hagen: a golf champion from 1914 to 1929.
2	4	Napoleon Bonaparte: The Emperor of France 1804 to 1814.
3	4	Elba: Italian island Napoleon was exiled to and escaped from in 1815.
4	4	St. Helena: British island where Napoleon was imprisoned after his brief reign as Emperor in 1815. He died from cancer there in 1821.
5	5	Bathtub Gin: slang term for homemade liquor.
6	7	Belladonna treatment: administration of the sedative and antispasmodic drug Belladonna; formerly used to relieve some of the effects of alcohol withdrawal.
7	8	Armistice Day: now known as Veterans Day.
8	12	Czar: former title of the ruler of Russia.

Chapter 2

THERE IS A SOLUTION

*W*E, OF ALCOHOLICS ANONYMOUS, know thousands of men and women who were once just as hopeless as Bill. Nearly all have recovered. They have solved the drink problem.

We are average Americans. All sections of this country and many of its occupations are represented, as well as many political, economic, social, and religious backgrounds. We are people who normally would not mix. But there exists among us a fellowship, a friendliness, and an understanding which is indescribably wonderful. We are like the passengers of a great liner the moment after rescue from shipwreck when camaraderie, joyousness and democracy pervade the vessel from steerage to Captain's table. Unlike the feelings of the ship's passengers, however, our joy in escape from disaster does not subside as we go our individual ways. The feeling of having shared in a common peril is one element in the powerful cement which binds us. But that in itself would never have held us together as we are now joined.

The tremendous fact for every one of us is that we have discovered a common solution. We have a way out on which we can absolutely agree, and upon which we can join in brotherly and harmonious action. This is the great news this book carries to those who suffer from alcoholism.

An illness of this sort—and we have come to believe it an illness—involves those about us in a way no other human sickness can. If a person has cancer all are sorry for him and no one is angry or hurt. But not so with the alcoholic illness, for with it there goes annihilation of all the things worth while in life. It engulfs all whose lives touch the sufferer's. It brings misunderstanding, fierce resentment, financial insecurity, disgusted friends and employers, warped lives of blameless children, sad wives and parents—anyone can increase the list.

We hope this volume will inform and comfort those who are, or who may be affected. There are many.

Highly competent psychiatrists who have dealt with us have found it sometimes impossible to persuade an alcoholic to discuss his situation without reserve. Strangely enough, wives, parents and intimate friends usually find us even more unapproachable than do the psychiatrist and the doctor.

But the ex-problem drinker who has found this solution, who is properly armed with facts about himself, can generally win the entire confidence of another alcoholic in a few hours. Until such an understanding is reached, little or nothing can be accomplished.

That the man who is making the approach has had the same difficulty, that he obviously knows what he is talking about, that his whole deportment shouts at the new prospect that he is a man with a real answer, that he has no attitude of Holier Than Thou, nothing whatever except the sincere desire to be helpful; that there are no fees to pay, no axes to grind, no people to please, no lectures to be endured—these are the conditions we have found most effective. After such an approach many take up their beds and walk again.

None of us makes a sole vocation of this work, nor do we think its effectiveness would be increased if we did. We feel that elimination of our drinking is but a beginning. A much more important demonstration of our principles lies before us in our respective homes, occupations and affairs. All of us spend much of our spare time in the sort of effort which we are going to describe. A few are fortunate enough to be so situated that they can give nearly all their time to the work.

If we keep on the way we are going there is little doubt that much good will result, but the surface of the problem would hardly be scratched. Those of us who live in large cities are overcome by the reflection that close by hundreds are dropping into oblivion every day. Many could recover if they had the opportunity we have enjoyed. How then shall we present that which has been so freely given us?

We have concluded to publish an anonymous volume setting forth the problem as we see it. We shall bring to the task our combined experience and knowledge. This should suggest a useful program for anyone concerned with a drinking problem.

Of necessity there will have to be discussion of matters medical, psychiatric, social, and religious. We are aware that these matters are, from their very nature, controversial. Nothing would please us so much as to write a book which would contain no basis for contention or argument. We shall do our utmost to achieve that ideal. Most of us sense that real tolerance of other people's shortcomings and viewpoints and a respect for their opinions are attitudes which make us more useful to others. Our very lives, as ex-problem drinkers, depend upon our constant thought of others and how we may help meet their needs.

You may already have asked yourself why it is that all of us became so very ill from drinking. Doubtless you are curious to discover how and why, in the face of expert opinion to the contrary, we have recovered from a hopeless condition of mind and body. If you are an alcoholic who wants to get over it, you may already be asking—"What do I have to do?"

It is the purpose of this book to answer such questions specifically. We shall tell you what we have done. Before going into a detailed discussion, it may be well to summarize some points as we see them.

How many times people have said to us:"I can take it or leave it alone. Why can't he?" "Why don't you drink like a gentleman or quit?" "That fellow can't handle his liquor." "Why don't you try beer and wine?" "Lay off the hard stuff." "His will power must be weak." "He could stop if he wanted to." "She's such a sweet girl, I should think he'd stop for her sake." "The doctor told him that if he ever drank again it would kill him, but there he is all lit up again."

Now these are commonplace observations on drinkers which we hear all the time. Back of them is a world of ignorance and misunderstanding. We see that these expressions refer to people whose reactions are very different from ours.

Moderate drinkers have little trouble in giving up liquor entirely if they have good reason for it. They can take it or leave it alone.

Then we have a certain type of hard drinker. He may have the habit badly enough to gradually impair him physically and mentally. It may cause him to die a few years before his time. If a sufficiently strong reason—ill health, falling in love, change of environment, or the warning of a doctor—becomes operative, this man can also stop or moderate, although he may find it difficult and troublesome and may even need medical attention.

But what about the real alcoholic? He may start off as a moderate drinker; he may or may not become a continous hard drinker; but at some stage of his drinking career he begins to lose all control of his liquor consumption, once he starts to drink.

Here is the fellow who has been puzzling you, especially in his lack of control. He does absurd, incredible, tragic things while drinking. He is a real Dr. Jekyll and Mr. Hyde.[1] He is seldom mildly intoxicated. He is always more or less insanely drunk. His disposition while drinking resembles his normal nature but little. He may be one of the finest fellows in the world. Yet let him drink for a day, and he frequently becomes disgustingly, and even dangerously anti-social. He has a positive genius for getting tight at exactly the wrong moment, particularly when some important decision must be made or engagement kept. He is often perfectly sensible and well balanced concerning everything except liquor, but in that respect he is incredibly dishonest and selfish. He often possesses special abilities, skills, and aptitudes, and has a promising career ahead of him. He uses his gifts to build up a bright outlook for his family and himself, and then pulls the structure down on his head by a senseless series of sprees. He is the fellow who goes to bed so intoxicated he ought to sleep the clock around. Yet early next morning he searches madly for the bottle he misplaced the night before. If he can afford it, he may have liquor concealed all over his house to be certain no one gets his entire supply away from him to throw down the wastepipe. As matters grow worse, he begins to use a combination of high-powered sedative and liquor to quiet his nerves so he can go to work. Then comes the day when he simply cannot make it and gets drunk all over again. Perhaps he goes to a doctor who gives him morphine or some sedative with which to taper off. Then he begins to appear at hospitals and sanitariums.

This is by no means a comprehensive picture of the true alcoholic, as our behavior patterns vary. But this description should identify him roughly.

Why does he behave like this? If hundreds of experiences have shown him that one drink means another debacle with all its attendant suffering and humiliation, why is it he takes that one drink? Why can't he stay on the water wagon? What has become of the common sense and will power that he still sometimes displays with respect to other matters?

Perhaps there never will be a full answer to these questions. Opinions vary considerably as to why the alcoholic reacts differently from normal people. We are not sure why, once a certain point is reached, little can be done for him. We cannot answer the riddle.

We know that while the alcoholic keeps away from drink, as he may do for months or years, he reacts much like other men. We are equally positive that once he takes any alcohol whatever into his system, something happens, both in the bodily and mental sense, which makes it virtually impossible for him to stop. The experience of any alcoholic will abundantly confirm this.

These observations would be academic and pointless if our friend never took the first drink, thereby setting the terrible cycle in motion. Therefore, the main problem of the alcoholic centers in his mind, rather than in his body. If you ask him why he started on that last bender, the chances are he will offer you any one of a hundred alibis. Sometimes these excuses have a certain plausibility, but none of them really makes sense in the light of the havoc an alcoholic's drinking bout creates. They sound like the philosophy of the man who, having a headache, beats himself on the head with a hammer so that he can't feel the ache. If you draw this fallacious reasoning to the attention of an alcoholic, he will laugh it off, or become irritated and refuse to talk.

Once in a while he may tell the truth. And the truth, strange to say, is usually that he has no more idea why he took that first drink than you have. Some drinkers have excuses with which they are satisfied part of the time. But in their hearts they really do not know why they do it. Once this malady has a real hold, they are a baffled lot. There is the obsession that somehow, someday, they will beat the game. But they often suspect they are down for the count.

How true this is, few realize. In a vague way their families and friends sense that these drinkers are abnormal, but everybody hopefully awaits the day when the sufferer will rouse himself from his lethargy and assert his power of will. The tragic truth is that if the man be a real alcoholic, the happy day may not arrive. He has lost control. At a certain point in the drinking of every alcoholic, he passes into a state where the most powerful desire to stop drinking is of absolutely no avail. This tragic situation has already arrived in practically every case long before it is suspected.

The fact is that most alcoholics, for reasons yet obscure, have lost the power of choice in drink. Our so-called will power becomes practically nonexistent. We are unable, at certain times, to bring into our consciousness with sufficient force the memory of the suffering and humiliation of even a week or a month ago. We are without defense against the first drink.

The almost certain consequences that follow taking even a glass of beer do not crowd into the mind to deter us. If these thoughts occur, they are hazy and readily supplanted with the old threadbare idea that this time we shall handle ourselves like other people. There is a complete failure of the kind of defense that keeps one from putting his hand on a hot stove.

The alcoholic may say to himself in the most casual way, "It won't burn me this time, so here's how!" Or perhaps he doesn't think at all. How often have some of us begun to drink in this nonchalant way, and after the third or fourth, pounded on the bar and said to ourselves, "For God's sake, how did I ever get started again?" Only to have that thought supplanted by "Well, I'll stop with the sixth drink." Or "What's the use anyhow?"

When this sort of thinking is fully established in an individual with alcoholic tendencies, he has probably placed himself beyond human aid, and unless locked up, may die or go permanently insane. These stark and ugly facts have been confirmed by legions of alcoholics throughout history. But for the grace of God, there would have been thousands more convincing demonstrations. So many want to stop but cannot.

There is a solution. Almost none of us liked the self-searching, the leveling of our pride, the confession of shortcomings which the process requires for its successful consummation. But we saw that it really worked in others, and we had come to believe in the hopelessness and futility of life as we had been living it. When, therefore, we were approached by those in whom the problem had been solved, there was nothing left for us but to pick up the simple kit of spiritual tools laid at our feet. We have found much of heaven and we have been rocketed into a fourth dimension of existence of which we had not even dreamed.

The great fact is just this, and nothing less: That we have had deep and effective spiritual experiences* which have revolutionized our whole attitude toward life, toward our fellows and toward God's universe. The central fact of our lives today is the absolute certainty that our Creator has entered into our hearts and lives in a way which is indeed miraculous. He has commenced to accomplish those things for us which we could never do by ourselves.

If you are as seriously alcoholic as we were, we believe there is no middle-of-the-road solution. We were in a position where life was becoming impossible, and if we had passed into the region from which there is no return through human aid, we had but two alternatives: One was to go on to the bitter end, blotting out the consciousness of our intolerable situation as best we could; and the other, to accept spiritual help. This

---

* see "Spiritual Experience."

we did because we honestly wanted to, and were willing to make the effort.

A certain American business man had ability, good sense, and high character. For years he had floundered from one sanitarium to another. He had consulted the best known American psychiatrists. Then he had gone to Europe, placing himself in the care of a celebrated physician (the psychiatrist, Dr. Jung) who prescribed for him. Though experience had made him skeptical, he finished his treatment with unusual confidence. His physical and mental condition were unusually good. Above all, he believed he had acquired such a profound knowledge of the inner workings of his mind and its hidden springs that relapse was unthinkable. Nevertheless, he was drunk in a short time. More baffling still, he could give himself no satisfactory explanation for his fall.

So he returned to this doctor, whom he admired, and asked him point-blank why he could not recover. He wished above all things to regain self-control. He seemed quite rational and well-balanced with respect to other problems. Yet he had no control whatever over alcohol. Why was this?

He begged the doctor to tell him the whole truth, and he got it. In the doctor's judgment he was utterly hopeless; he could never regain his position in society and he would have to place himself under lock and key or hire a bodyguard if he expected to live long. That was a great physician's opinion.

But this man still lives, and is a free man. He does not need a bodyguard nor is he confined. He can go anywhere on this earth where other free men may go without disaster, provided he remains willing to maintain a certain simple attitude.

Some of our alcoholic readers may think they can do without spiritual help. Let us tell you the rest of the conversation our friend had with his doctor.

The doctor said: "You have the mind of a chronic alcoholic. I have never seen one single case recover, where that state of mind existed to the extent that it does in you." Our friend felt as though the gates of hell had closed on him with a clang.

He said to the doctor, "Is there no exception?"

"Yes," replied the doctor," there is. Exceptions to cases such as yours have been occurring since early times. Here and there, once in a while, alcoholics have had what are called vital spiritual experiences. To me these occurrences are phenomena. They appear to be in the nature of huge emotional displacements and rearrangements. Ideas, emotions, and attitudes which were once the guiding forces of the lives of these men are suddenly cast to one side, and a completely new set of conceptions and motives begin to dominate them. In fact, I have been trying to produce some such emotional rearrangement within you. With many individuals the methods which I employed are successful, but I have never been successful with an alcoholic of your description."*

Upon hearing this, our friend was somewhat relieved, for he reflected that, after all, he was a good church member. This hope, however, was destroyed by the doctor's telling him that while his religious convictions were very good, in his case they did not spell the necessary vital spiritual experience.

* see "Spiritual Experience."

Here was the terrible dilemma in which our friend found himself when he had the extraordinary experience, which as we have already told you, made him a free man.

We, in our turn, sought the same escape with all the desperation of drowning men. What seemed at first a flimsy reed, has proved to be the loving and powerful hand of God. A new life has been given us or, if you prefer, "a design for living" that really works.

The distinguished American psychologist, William James, in his book "Varieties of Religious Experience," indicates a multitude of ways in which men have discovered God. We have no desire to convince anyone that there is only one way by which faith can be acquired. If what we have learned and felt and seen means anything at all, it means that all of us, whatever our race, creed, or color are the children of a living Creator with whom we may form a relationship upon simple and understandable terms as soon as we are willing and honest enough to try. Those having religious affiliations will find here nothing disturbing to their beliefs or ceremonies. There is no friction among us over such matters.

We think it no concern of ours what religious bodies our members identify themselves with as individuals. This should be an entirely personal affair which each one decides for himself in the light of past associations, or his present choice. Not all of us join religious bodies, but most of us favor such memberships.

In the following chapter, there appears an explanation of alcoholism, as we understand it, then a chapter addressed to the agnostic. Many who once were in this class are now among our members. Surprisingly enough, we find such convictions no great obstacle to a spiritual experience.

Further on, clear-cut directions are given showing how we recovered. These are followed by forty-three personal experiences.

Each individual, in the personal stories, describes in his own language and from his own point of view the way he established his relationship with God. These give a fair cross section of our membership and a clear-cut idea of what has actually happened in their lives.

We hope no one will consider these self-revealing accounts in bad taste. Our hope is that many alcoholic men and women, desperately in need, will see these pages, and we believe that it is only by fully disclosing ourselves and our problems that they will be persuaded to say, "Yes, I am one of them too; I must have this thing."

Note	Page	
1	21	Dr. Jekyll and Mr. Hyde: literary reference to describe a person with a split personality - one good and the other bad.

Chapter 3

MORE ABOUT ALCOHOLISM

*M*OST OF us have been unwilling to admit we were real alcoholics. No person likes to think he is bodily and mentally different from his fellows. Therefore, it is not surprising that our drinking careers have been characterized by countless vain attempts to prove we could drink like other people. The idea that somehow, someday he will control and enjoy his drinking is the great obsession of every abnormal drinker. The persistence of this illusion is astonishing. Many pursue it into the gates of insanity or death.

We learned that we had to fully concede to our innermost selves that we were alcoholics. This is the first step in recovery. The delusion that we are like other people, or presently may be, has to be smashed.

We alcoholics are men and women who have lost the ability to control our drinking. We know that no real alcoholic *ever* recovers control. All of us felt at times that we were regaining control, but such intervals—usually brief—were inevitably followed by still less control, which led in time to pitiful and incomprehensible demoralization. We are convinced to a man that alcoholics of our type are in the grip of a progressive illness. Over any considerable period we get worse, never better.

We are like men who have lost their legs; they never grow new ones. Neither does there appear to be any kind of treatment which will make alcoholics of our kind like other men. We have tried every imaginable remedy. In some instances there has been brief recovery, followed always by a still worse relapse. Physicians who are familiar with alcoholism agree there is no such thing as making a normal drinker out of an alcoholic. Science may one day accomplish this, but it hasn't done so yet.

Despite all we can say, many who are real alcoholics are not going to believe they are in that class. By every form of self-deception and experimentation, they will try to prove themselves exceptions to the rule, therefore nonalcoholic. If anyone who is showing inability to control his drinking can do the right- about-face and drink like a gentleman, our hats are off to him. Heaven knows, we have tried hard enough and long enough to drink like other people!

Here are some of the methods we have tried: Drinking beer only, limiting the number of drinks, never drinking alone, never drinking in the morning, drinking only at home, never having it in the house, never drinking during business hours, drinking only at parties, switching from scotch to brandy, drinking only natural wines, agreeing to resign if ever drunk on the job, taking a trip, not taking a trip, swearing off forever (with and without a solemn oath), taking more physical exercise, reading inspirational books, going to health farms and sanitariums, accepting voluntary commitment to asylums—we could increase the list ad infinitum.

We do not like to pronounce any individual as alcoholic, but you can quickly diagnose yourself. Step over to the nearest barroom and try some controlled drinking. Try to drink and stop abruptly. Try it

more than once. It will not take long for you to decide,
if you are honest with yourself about it. It may be worth
a bad case of jitters if you get a full knowledge of your
condition.

Though there is no way of proving it, we believe
that early in our drinking careers most of us could
have stopped drinking. But the difficulty is that few
alcoholics have enough desire to stop while there is
yet time. We have heard of a few instances where
people, who showed definite signs of alcoholism,
were able to stop for a long period because of an over-
powering desire to do so. Here is one.

A man of thirty was doing a great deal of spree
drinking. He was very nervous in the morning after
these bouts and quieted himself with more liquor. He
was ambitious to succeed in business, but saw that he
would get nowhere if he drank at all. Once he started,
he had no control whatever. He made up his mind that
until he had been successful in business and had retired,
he would not touch another drop. An exceptional man,
he remained bone dry for twenty-five years and retired
at the age of fifty-five, after a successful and happy business career. Then he fell victim to a belief which practically every alcoholic has—that his long period of sobriety and self-discipline had qualified him to drink as
other men. Out came his carpet slippers and a bottle. In
two months he was in a hospital, puzzled and humiliated.
He tried to regulate his drinking for a while, making several trips to the hospital meantime. Then, gathering all his
forces, he attempted to stop altogether and found he could
not. Every means of solving his problem which

money could buy was at his disposal. Every attempt failed. Though a robust man at retirement, he went to pieces quickly and was dead within four years.

This case contains a powerful lesson. Most of us have believed that if we remained sober for a long stretch, we could thereafter drink normally. But here is a man who at fifty-five years found he was just where he had left off at thirty. We have seen the truth demonstrated again and again: "Once an alcoholic, always an alcoholic." Commencing to drink after a period of sobriety, we are in a short time as bad as ever. If we are planning to stop drinking, there must be no reservation of any kind, nor any lurking notion that someday we will be immune to alcohol.

Young people may be encouraged by this man's experience to think that they can stop, as he did, on their own will power. We doubt if many of them can do it, because none will really want to stop, and hardly one of them, because of the peculiar mental twist already acquired, will find he can win out. Several of our crowd, men of thirty or less, had been drinking only a few years, but they found themselves as helpless as those who had been drinking twenty years.

To be gravely affected, one does not necessarily have to drink a long time nor take the quantities some of us have. This is particularly true of women. Potential female alcoholics often turn into the real thing and are gone beyond recall in a few years. Certain drinkers, who would be greatly insulted if called alcoholics, are astonished at their inability to stop. We, who are familiar with the symptoms, see large numbers of potential alcoholics among young people everywhere. But try and get them to see it!*

As we look back, we feel we had gone on drinking many years beyond the point where we could quit on our will power. If anyone questions whether he has entered this dangerous area, let him try leaving liquor alone for one year. If he is a real alcoholic and very far advanced, there is scant chance of success. In the early days of our drinking we occasionally remained sober for a year or more, becoming serious drinkers again later. Though you may be able to stop for a considerable period, you may yet be a potential alcoholic. We think few, to whom this book will appeal, can stay dry anything like a year. Some will be drunk the day after making their resolutions; most of them within a few weeks.

For those who are unable to drink moderately the question is how to stop altogether. We are assuming, of course, that the reader desires to stop. Whether such a person can quit upon a nonspiritual basis depends upon the extent to which he has already lost the power to choose whether he will drink or not. Many of us felt that we had plenty of character. There was a tremendous urge to cease forever. Yet we found it impossible. This is the baffling feature of alcoholism as we know it—this utter inability to leave it alone, no matter how great the necessity or the wish.

How then shall we help our readers determine, to their own satisfaction, whether they are one of us? The experiment of quitting for a period of time will be helpful, but we think we can render an even greater service to alcoholic sufferers and perhaps to the med-

* True when this book was first published. In 1993 a membership survey showed that one-fifth of A.A.s were 30 years and under.

ical fraternity. So we shall describe some of the mental states that precede a relapse into drinking, for obviously this is the crux of the problem.

What sort of thinking dominates an alcoholic who repeats time after time the desperate experiment of the first drink? Friends who have reasoned with him after a spree which has brought him to the point of divorce or bankruptcy are mystified when he walks directly into a saloon. Why does he? Of what is he thinking?

Our first example is a friend we shall call Jim. This man has a charming wife and family. He inherited a lucrative automobile agency. He had a commendable World War record. He is a good salesman. Everybody likes him. He is an intelligent man, normal so far as we can see, except for a nervous disposition. He did no drinking until he was thirty-five. In a few years he became so violent when intoxicated that he had to be committed. On leaving the asylum he came into contact with us.

We told him what we knew of alcoholism and the answer we had found. He made a beginning. His family was re-assembled, and he began to work as a salesman for the business he had lost through drinking. All went well for a time, but he failed to enlarge his spiritual life. To his consternation, he found himself drunk half a dozen times in rapid succession. On each of these occasions we worked with him, reviewing carefully what had happened. He agreed he was a real alcoholic and in a serious condition. He knew he faced another trip to the asylum if he kept on. Moreover, he would lose his family for whom he had a deep affection.

Yet he got drunk again. We asked him to tell us exactly how it happened. This is his story: "I came to work on Tuesday morning. I remember I felt irritated that I had to be a salesman for a concern I once owned. I had a few words with the boss, but nothing serious. Then I decided to drive into the country and see one of my prospects for a car. On the way I felt hungry so I stopped at a roadside place where they have a bar. I had no intention of drinking. I just thought I would get a sandwich. I also had the notion that I might find a customer for a car at this place, which was familiar for I had been going to it for years. I had eaten there many times during the months I was sober. I sat down at a table and ordered a sandwich and a glass of milk. Still no thought of drinking. I ordered another sandwich and decided to have another glass of milk.

"Suddenly the thought crossed my mind that if I were to put an ounce of whiskey in my milk it couldn't hurt me on a full stomach. I ordered a whiskey and poured it into the milk. I vaguely sensed I was not being any too smart, but felt reassured as I was taking the whiskey on a full stomach. The experiment went so well that I ordered another whiskey and poured it into more milk. That didn't seem to bother me so I tried another."

Thus started one more journey to the asylum for Jim. Here was the threat of commitment, the loss of family and position, to say nothing of that intense mental and physical suffering which drinking always caused him. *He had much knowledge about himself as an alcoholic. Yet all reasons for not drinking were easily pushed aside in favor of the foolish idea that he could take whiskey if only he mixed it with milk!*

Whatever the precise definition of the word may be, we call this plain insanity. How can such a lack of proportion, of the ability to think straight, be called anything else?

You may think this an extreme case. To us it is not far-fetched, for this kind of thinking has been characteristic of every single one of us. We have sometimes reflected more than Jim did upon the consequences. But there was always the curious mental phenomenon that parallel with our sound reasoning there inevitably ran some insanely trivial excuse for taking the first drink. Our sound reasoning failed to hold us in check. The insane idea won out. Next day we would ask ourselves, in all earnestness and sincerity, how it could have happened.

In some circumstances we have gone out deliberately to get drunk, feeling ourselves justified by nervousness, anger, worry, depression, jealousy or the like. But even in this type of beginning we are obliged to admit that our justification for a spree was insanely insufficient in the light of what always happened. We now see that when we began to drink deliberately, instead of casually, there was little serious or effective thought during the period of premeditation of what the terrific consequences might be.

Our behavior is as absurd and incomprehensible with respect to the first drink as that of an individual with a passion, say, for jay-walking. He gets a thrill out of skipping in front of fast-moving vehicles. He enjoys himself for a few years in spite of friendly warnings. Up to this point you would label him as a foolish chap having queer ideas of fun. Luck then deserts him and he is slightly injured several times in succession. You would expect him, if he were normal, to cut it out. Presently he is hit again and this time has a fractured skull. Within a week after leaving the hospital a fast-moving trolley car breaks his arm. He tells you he has decided to stop jay-walking for good, but in a few weeks he breaks both legs.

On through the years this conduct continues, accompanied by his continual promises to be careful or to keep off the streets altogether. Finally, he can no longer work, his wife gets a divorce and he is held up to ridicule. He tries every known means to get the jay-walking idea out of his head. He shuts himself up in an asylum, hoping to mend his ways. But the day he comes out he races in front of a fire engine, which breaks his back. Such a man would be crazy, wouldn't he?

You may think our illustration is too ridiculous. But is it? We, who have been through the wringer, have to admit if we substituted alcoholism for jay-walking, the illustration would fit us exactly. However intelligent we may have been in other respects, where alcohol has been involved, we have been strangely insane. It's strong language—but isn't it true?

Some of you are thinking: "Yes, what you tell us is true, but it doesn't fully apply. We admit we have some of these symptoms, but we have not gone to the extremes you fellows did, nor are we likely to, for we understand ourselves so well after what you have told us that such things cannot happen again. We have not lost everything in life through drinking and we certainly do not intend to. Thanks for the information."

That may be true of certain nonalcoholic people who, though drinking foolishly and heavily at the present time, are able to stop or moderate, because their brains and bodies have not been damaged as ours were. But the actual or potential alcoholic, with hardly an exception, will be *absolutely unable to stop drinking on the basis of self-knowledge.* This is a point we wish to emphasize and re-emphasize, to smash home upon our alcoholic readers as it has been revealed to us out of bitter experience. Let us take another illustration.

Fred is partner in a well known accounting firm. His income is good, he has a fine home, is happily married and the father of promising children of college age. He has so attractive a personality that he makes friends with everyone. If ever there was a successful business man, it is Fred. To all appearance he is a stable, well balanced individual. Yet, he is alcoholic. We first saw Fred about a year ago in a hospital where he had gone to recover from a bad case of jitters. It was his first experience of this kind, and he was much ashamed of it. Far from admitting he was an alcoholic, he told himself he came to the hospital to rest his nerves. The doctor intimated strongly that he might be worse than he realized. For a few days he was depressed about his condition. He made up his mind to quit drinking altogether. It never occurred to him that perhaps he could not do so, in spite of his character and standing. Fred would not believe himself an alcoholic, much less accept a spiritual remedy for his problem. We told him what we knew about alcoholism. He was interested and conceded that he had some of the symptoms, but he was a long way from admitting that he could do nothing about it himself. He was positive that this humiliating experience, plus the knowledge he had acquired, would keep him sober the rest of his life. Self-knowledge would fix it.

We heard no more of Fred for a while. One day we were told that he was back in the hospital. This time he was quite shaky. He soon indicated he was anxious to see us. The story he told is most instructive, for here was a chap absolutely convinced he had to stop drinking, who had no excuse for drinking, who exhibited splendid judgment and determination in all his other concerns, yet was flat on his back nevertheless.

Let him tell you about it: "I was much impressed with what you fellows said about alcoholism, and I frankly did not believe it would be possible for me to drink again. I rather appreciated your ideas about the subtle insanity which precedes the first drink, but I was confident it could not happen to me after what I had learned. I reasoned I was not so far advanced as most of you fellows, that I had been usually successful in licking my other personal problems, and that I would therefore be successful where you men failed. I felt I had every right to be self-confident, that it would be only a matter of exercising my will power and keeping on guard.

"In this frame of mind, I went about my business and for a time all was well. I had no trouble refusing drinks, and began to wonder if I had not been making too hard work of a simple matter. One day I went to Washington to present some accounting evidence to a government bureau. I had been out of town before during this particular dry spell, so there was nothing new about that. Physically, I felt fine. Neither did I have any pressing problems or worries. My business came off well, I was pleased and knew my partners would be too. It was the end of a perfect day, not a cloud on the horizon.

"I went to my hotel and leisurely dressed for dinner. *As I crossed the threshold of the dining room, the thought came to mind that it would be nice to have a couple of cocktails with dinner. That was all. Nothing more.* I ordered a cocktail and my meal. Then I ordered another cocktail. After dinner I decided to take a walk. When I returned to the hotel it struck me a highball would be fine before going to bed, so I stepped into the bar and had one. I remember having several more that night and plenty next morning. I have a shadowy recollection of being in an airplane bound for New York and of finding a friendly taxicab driver at the landing field instead of my wife. The driver escorted me about for several days. I know little of where I went or what I said and did. Then came the hospital with unbearable mental and physical suffering.

"As soon as I regained my ability to think, I went carefully over that evening in Washington. *Not only had I been off guard, I had made no fight whatever against the first drink. This time I had not thought of the consequences at all.* I had commenced to drink as carelessly as though the cocktails were ginger ale. I now remembered what my alcoholic friends had told me, how they prophesied that if I had an alcoholic mind, the time and place would come—I would drink again. They had said that though I did raise a defense, it would one day give way before some trivial reason for having a drink. Well, just that did happen and more, for what I had learned of alcoholism did not occur to me at all. I knew from that moment that I had an alcoholic mind. I saw that will power and self-knowledge would not help in those strange mental blank spots. I had never been able to understand people who said that a problem had them hopelessly defeated. I knew then. It was a crushing blow.

"Two of the members of Alcoholics Anonymous came to see me. They grinned, which I didn't like so much, and then asked me if I thought myself alcoholic and if I were really licked this time. I had to concede both propositions. They piled on me heaps of evidence to the effect that an alcoholic mentality, such as I had exhibited in Washington, was a hopeless condition. They cited cases out of their own experience by the dozen. This process snuffed out the last flicker of conviction that I could do the job myself.

"Then they outlined the spiritual answer and program of action which a hundred of them had followed successfully. Though I had been only a nominal churchman, their proposals were not, intellectually, hard to swallow. But the program of action, though entirely sensible, was pretty drastic. It meant I would have to throw several lifelong conceptions out of the window. That was not easy. But the moment I made up my mind to go through with the process, I had the curious feeling that my alcoholic condition was relieved, as in fact it proved to be.

"Quite as important was the discovery that spiritual principles would solve all my problems. I have since been brought into a way of living infinitely more satisfying and, I hope, more useful than the life I lived before. My old manner of life was by no means a bad one, but I would not exchange its best moments for the worst I have now. I would not go back to it even if I could."

Fred's story speaks for itself. We hope it strikes home to thousands like him. He had felt only the first nip of the wringer. Most alcoholics have to be pretty badly mangled before they really commence to solve their problems.

Many doctors and psychiatrists agree with our conclusions. One of these men, staff member of a world-renowned hospital, recently made this statement to some of us: "What you say about the general hopelessness of the average alcoholic's plight is, in my opinion, correct. As to two of you men, whose stories I have heard, there is no doubt in my mind that you were 100% hopeless, apart from divine help. Had you offered yourselves as patients at this hospital, I would not have taken you, if I had been able to avoid it. People like you are too heartbreaking. Though not a religious person, I have profound respect for the spiritual approach in such cases as yours. For most cases, there is virtually no other solution."

Once more: The alcoholic at certain times has no effective mental defense against the first drink. Except in a few rare cases, neither he nor any other human being can provide such a defense. His defense must come from a Higher Power.

Chapter 4

WE AGNOSTICS

I N THE PRECEDING chapters you have learned something of alcoholism. We hope we have made clear the distinction between the alcoholic and the nonalcoholic. If, when you honestly want to, you find you cannot quit entirely, or if when drinking, you have little control over the amount you take, you are probably alcoholic. If that be the case, you may be suffering from an illness which only a spiritual experience will conquer.

To one who feels he is an atheist or agnostic such an experience seems impossible, but to continue as he is means disaster, especially if he is an alcoholic of the hopeless variety. To be doomed to an alcoholic death or to live on a spiritual basis are not always easy alternatives to face.

But it isn't so difficult. About half our original fellowship were of exactly that type. At first some of us tried to avoid the issue, hoping against hope we were not true alcoholics. But after a while we had to face the fact that we must find a spiritual basis of life—or else. Perhaps it is going to be that way with you. But cheer up, something like half of us thought we were atheists or agnostics. Our experience shows that you need not be disconcerted.

If a mere code of morals or a better philosophy of life were sufficient to overcome alcoholism, many of us would have recovered long ago. But we found that such codes and philosophies did not save us, no matter how much we tried. We could wish to be moral, we could wish to be philosophically comforted, in fact, we could will these things with all our might, but the needed power wasn't there. Our human resources, as marshalled by the will, were not sufficient; they failed utterly.

Lack of power, that was our dilemma. We had to find a power by which we could live, and it had to be a *Power greater than ourselves.* Obviously. But where and how were we to find this Power?

Well, that's exactly what this book is about. Its main object is to enable you to find a Power greater than yourself which will solve your problem. That means we have written a book which we believe to be spiritual as well as moral. And it means, of course, that we are going to talk about God. Here difficulty arises with agnostics. Many times we talk to a new man and watch his hope rise as we discuss his alcoholic problems and explain our fellowship. But his face falls when we speak of spiritual matters, especially when we mention God, for we have re-opened a subject which our man thought he had neatly evaded or entirely ignored.

We know how he feels. We have shared his honest doubt and prejudice. Some of us have been violently anti-religious. To others, the word "God" brought up a particular idea of Him with which someone had tried to impress them during childhood. Perhaps we rejected this particular conception because it seemed inadequate. With that rejection we imagined we had abandoned the God idea entirely. We were bothered with the thought that faith and dependence upon a Power beyond ourselves was somewhat weak, even cowardly. We looked upon this world of warring individuals, warring theological systems, and inexplicable calamity, with deep skepticism. We looked askance at many individuals who claimed to be godly. How could a Supreme Being have anything to do with it all? And who could comprehend a Supreme Being anyhow? Yet, in other moments, we found ourselves thinking, when enchanted by a starlit night, "Who, then, made all this?" There was a feeling of awe and wonder, but it was fleeting and soon lost.

Yes, we of agnostic temperament have had these thoughts and experiences. Let us make haste to reassure you. We found that as soon as we were able to lay aside prejudice and express even a willingness to believe in a Power greater than ourselves, we commenced to get results, even though it was impossible for any of us to fully define or comprehend that Power, which is God.

Much to our relief, we discovered we did not need to consider another's conception of God. Our own conception, however inadequate, was sufficient to make the approach and to effect a contact with Him. As soon as we admitted the possible existence of a Creative Intelligence, a Spirit of the Universe underlying the totality of things, we began to be possessed of a new sense of power and direction, provided we took other simple steps. We found that God does not make too hard terms with those who seek Him. To us, the Realm of Spirit is broad, roomy, all inclusive; never exclusive or forbidding to those who earnestly seek. It is open, we believe, to all men.

When, therefore, we speak to you of God, we mean your own conception of God. This applies, too, to other spiritual expressions which you find in this book. Do not let any prejudice you may have against spiritual terms deter you from honestly asking yourself what they mean to you. At the start, this was all we needed to commence spiritual growth, to effect our first conscious relation with God as we understood Him. Afterward, we found ourselves accepting many things which then seemed entirely out of reach. That was growth, but if we wished to grow we had to begin somewhere. So we used our own conception, however limited it was.

We needed to ask ourselves but one short question. "Do I now believe, or am I even willing to believe, that there is a Power greater than myself?" As soon as a man can say that he does believe, or is willing to believe, we emphatically assure him that he is on his way. It has been repeatedly proven among us that upon this simple cornerstone a wonderfully effective spiritual structure can be built.*

That was great news to us, for we had assumed we could not make use of spiritual principles unless we accepted many things on faith which seemed difficult to believe. When people presented us with spiritual approaches, how frequently did we all say, "I wish I had what that man has. I'm sure it would work if I could only believe as he believes. But I cannot accept as surely true the many articles of faith which are so plain to him." So it was comforting to learn that we could commence at a simpler level.

Besides a seeming inability to accept much on faith,

* Please be sure to read "Spiritual Experience."

we often found ourselves handicapped by obstinacy, sensitiveness, and unreasoning prejudice. Many of us have been so touchy that even casual reference to spiritual things made us bristle with antagonism. This sort of thinking had to be abandoned. Though some of us resisted, we found no great difficulty in casting aside such feelings. Faced with alcoholic destruction, we soon became as open minded on spiritual matters as we had tried to be on other questions. In this respect alcohol was a great persuader. It finally beat us into a state of reasonableness. Sometimes this was a tedious process; we hope no one else will be prejudiced for as long as some of us were.

The reader may still ask why he should believe in a Power greater than himself. We think there are good reasons. Let us have a look at some of them.

The practical individual of today is a stickler for facts and results. Nevertheless, the twentieth century readily accepts theories of all kinds, provided they are firmly grounded in fact. We have numerous theories, for example, about electricity. Everybody believes them without a murmur of doubt. Why this ready acceptance? Simply because it is impossible to explain what we see, feel, direct, and use, without a reasonable assumption as a starting point.

Everybody nowadays, believes in scores of assumptions for which there is good evidence, but no perfect visual proof. And does not science demonstrate that visual proof is the weakest proof? It is being constantly revealed, as mankind studies the material world, that outward appearances are not inward reality at all. To illustrate:

The prosaic steel girder is a mass of electrons whirling around each other at incredible speed. These tiny bodies are governed by precise laws, and these laws hold true throughout the material world. Science tells us so. We have no reason to doubt it. When, however, the perfectly logical assumption is suggested that underneath the material world and life as we see it, there is an All Powerful, Guiding, Creative Intelligence, right there our perverse streak comes to the surface and we laboriously set out to convince ourselves it isn't so. We read wordy books and indulge in windy arguments, thinking we believe this universe needs no God to explain it. Were our contentions true, it would follow that life originated out of nothing, means nothing, and proceeds nowhere.

Instead of regarding ourselves as intelligent agents, spearheads of God's ever advancing Creation, we agnostics and atheists chose to believe that our human intelligence was the last word, the alpha and the omega, the beginning and end of all. Rather vain of us, wasn't it?

We, who have traveled this dubious path, beg you to lay aside prejudice, even against organized religion. We have learned that whatever the human frailties of various faiths may be, those faiths have given purpose and direction to millions. People of faith have a logical idea of what life is all about. Actually, we used to have no reasonable conception whatever. We used to amuse ourselves by cynically dissecting spiritual beliefs and practices when we might have observed that many spiritually-minded persons of all races, colors, and creeds were demonstrating a degree of stability, happiness and usefulness which we should have sought ourselves.

Instead, we looked at the human defects of these people, and sometimes used their shortcomings as a basis of wholesale condemnation. We talked of intolerance, while we were intolerant ourselves. We missed the reality and the beauty of the forest because we were diverted by the ugliness of some of its trees. We never gave the spiritual side of life a fair hearing.

In our personal stories you will find a wide variation in the way each teller approaches and conceives of the Power which is greater than himself. Whether we agree with a particular approach or conception seems to make little difference. Experience has taught us that these are matters about which, for our purpose, we need not be worried. They are questions for each individual to settle for himself.

On one proposition, however, these men and women are strikingly agreed. Every one of them has gained access to, and believes in, a Power greater than himself. This Power has in each case accomplished the miraculous, the humanly impossible. As a celebrated American statesman put it, "Let's look at the record."

Here are thousands of men and women, worldly indeed. They flatly declare that since they have come to believe in a Power greater than themselves, to take a certain attitude toward that Power, and to do certain simple things, there has been a revolutionary change in their way of living and thinking. In the face of collapse and despair, in the face of the total failure of their human resources, they found that a new power, peace, happiness, and sense of direction flowed into them. This happened soon after they wholeheartedly met a few simple requirements. Once confused and baffled by the seeming futility of existence, they show the underlying reasons why they were making heavy going of life. Leaving aside the drink question, they tell why living was so unsatisfactory. They show how the change came over them. When many hundreds of people are able to say that the consciousness of the Presence of God is today the most important fact of their lives, they present a powerful reason why one should have faith.

This world of ours has made more material progress in the last century than in all the millenniums which went before. Almost everyone knows the reason. Students of ancient history tell us that the intellect of men in those days was equal to the best of today. Yet in ancient times material progress was painfully slow. The spirit of modern scientific inquiry, research and invention was almost unknown. In the realm of the material, men's minds were fettered by superstition, tradition, and all sorts of fixed ideas. Some of the contemporaries of Columbus thought a round earth preposterous.[1] Others came near putting Galileo to death for his astronomical heresies.[2]

We asked ourselves this: Are not some of us just as biased and unreasonable about the realm of the spirit as were the ancients about the realm of the material? Even in the present century, American newspapers were afraid to print an account of the Wright brothers' first successful flight at Kitty Hawk.[3] Had not all efforts at flight failed before? Did not Professor Langley's flying machine go to the bottom of the Potomac River? Was it not true that the best mathematical minds had proved man could never fly? Had not people said God had reserved this privilege to the birds? Only thirty years later the conquest of the air was almost an old story and airplane travel was in full swing.

But in most fields our generation has witnessed complete liberation of our thinking. Show any longshoreman a Sunday supplement describing a proposal to explore the moon by means of a rocket and he will say "I bet they do it — maybe not so long either." Is not our age characterized by the ease with which we discard old ideas for new, by the complete readiness with which we throw away the theory or gadget which does not work for something new which does?

We had to ask ourselves why we shouldn't apply to our human problems this same readiness to change our point of view. We were having trouble with personal relationships, we couldn't control our emotional natures, we were a prey to misery and depression, we couldn't make a living, we had a feeling of uselessness, we were full of fear, we were unhappy, we couldn't seem to be of real help to other people — was not a basic solution of these bedevilments more important than whether we should see newsreels of lunar flight? Of course it was.

When we saw others solve their problems by a simple reliance upon the Spirit of the Universe, we had to stop doubting the power of God. Our ideas did not work. But the God idea did.

The Wright brothers' almost childish faith that they could build a machine which would fly was the mainspring of their accomplishment. Without that, nothing could have happened. We agnostics and atheists were sticking to the idea that self-sufficiency would solve our problems. When others showed us that "God-sufficiency" worked with them, we began to feel like those who had insisted the Wrights would never fly.

Logic is great stuff. We liked it. We still like it. It is not by chance we were given the power to reason, to examine the evidence of our senses, and to draw conclusions. That is one of man's magnificent attributes. We agnostically inclined would not feel satisfied with a proposal which does not lend itself to reasonable approach and interpretation. Hence we are at pains to tell why we think our present faith is reasonable, why we think it more sane and logical to believe than not to believe, why we say our former thinking was soft and mushy when we threw up our hands in doubt and said, "We don't know."

When we became alcoholics, crushed by a self-imposed crisis we could not postpone or evade, we had to fearlessly face the proposition that either God is everything or else He is nothing. God either is, or He isn't. What was our choice to be?

Arrived at this point, we were squarely confronted with the question of faith. We couldn't duck the issue. Some of us had already walked far over the Bridge of Reason toward the desired shore of faith. The outlines and the promise of the New Land had brought lustre to tired eyes and fresh courage to flagging spirits. Friendly hands had stretched out in welcome. We were grateful that Reason had brought us so far. But somehow, we couldn't quite step ashore. Perhaps we had been leaning too heavily on Reason that last mile and we did not like to lose our support.

That was natural, but let us think a little more closely. Without knowing it, had we not been brought to where we stood by a certain kind of faith? For did we not believe in our own reasoning? Did we not have confidence in our ability to think? What was that but a sort of faith? Yes, we had been faithful, abjectly faithful to the God of Reason. So, in one way or another, we discovered that faith had been involved all the time!

We found, too, that we had been worshippers. What a state of mental goose-flesh that used to bring on! Had we not variously worshipped people, sentiment, things, money, and ourselves? And then, with a better motive, had we not worshipfully beheld the sunset, the sea, or a flower? Who of us had not loved something or somebody? How much did these feelings, these loves, these worships, have to do with pure reason? Little or nothing, we saw at last. Were not these things the tissue out of which our lives were constructed? Did not these feelings, after all, determine the course of our existence? It was impossible to say we had no capacity for faith, or love, or worship. In one form or another we had been living by faith and little else.

Imagine life without faith! Were nothing left but pure reason, it wouldn't be life. But we believed in life — of course we did. We could not prove life in the sense that you can prove a straight line is the shortest distance between two points, yet, there it was. Could we still say the whole thing was nothing but a mass of electrons, created out of nothing, meaning nothing, whirling on to a destiny of nothingness? Of course we couldn't. The electrons themselves seemed more intelligent than that. At least, so the chemist said.

Hence, we saw that reason isn't everything. Neither is reason, as most of us use it, entirely dependable, though it emanate from our best minds. What about people who proved that man could never fly?

Yet we had been seeing another kind of flight, a spiritual liberation from this world, people who rose above their problems. They said God made these things possible, and we only smiled. We had seen spiritual release, but liked to tell ourselves it wasn't true.

Actually we were fooling ourselves, for deep down in every man, woman, and child, is the fundamental idea of God. It may be obscured by calamity, by pomp, by worship of other things, but in some form or other it is there. For faith in a Power greater than ourselves, and miraculous demonstrations of that power in human lives, are facts as old as man himself.

We finally saw that faith in some kind of God was a part of our make-up, just as much as the feeling we have for a friend. Sometimes we had to search fearlessly, but He was there. He was as much a fact as we were. We found the Great Reality deep down within us. In the last analysis it is only there that He may be found. It was so with us.

We can only clear the ground a bit. If our testimony helps sweep away prejudice, enables you to think honestly, encourages you to search diligently within yourself, then, if you wish, you can join us on the Broad Highway. With this attitude you cannot fail. The consciousness of your belief is sure to come to you.

In this book you will read the experience of a man who thought he was an atheist. His story is so interesting that some of it should be told now. His change of heart was dramatic, convincing, and moving.

Our friend was a minister's son. He attended church school, where he became rebellious at what he thought an overdose of religious education. For years thereafter he was dogged by trouble and frustration. Business failure, insanity, fatal illness, suicide — these calamities in his immediate family embittered and depressed him. Post-war disillusionment, ever more serious alcoholism, impending mental and physical collapse, brought him to the point of self-destruction.

One night, when confined in a hospital, he was approached by an alcoholic who had known a spiritual experience. Our friend's gorge rose as he bitterly cried out: "If there is a God, He certainly hasn't done anything for me!" But later, alone in his room, he asked himself this question: "Is it possible that all the religious people I have known are wrong?" While pondering the answer he felt as though he lived in hell. Then, like a thunderbolt, a great thought came. It crowded out all else:

"Who are you to say there is no God?"

This man recounts that he tumbled out of bed to his knees. In a few seconds he was overwhelmed by a conviction of the Presence of God. It poured over and through him with the certainty and majesty of a great tide at flood. The barriers he had built through the years were swept away. He stood in the Presence of Infinite Power and Love. He had stepped from bridge to shore. For the first time, he lived in conscious companionship with his Creator.

Thus was our friend's cornerstone fixed in place. No later vicissitude has shaken it. His alcoholic problem was taken away. That very night, years ago, it disappeared. Save for a few brief moments of temptation the thought of drink has never returned; and at such times a great revulsion has risen up in him. Seemingly he could not drink even if he would. God had restored his sanity.

What is this but a miracle of healing? Yet its elements are simple. Circumstances made him willing to believe. He humbly offered himself to his Maker — then he knew.

Even so has God restored us all to our right minds. To this man, the revelation was sudden. Some of us grow into it more slowly. But He has come to all who have honestly sought Him.

When we drew near to Him He disclosed Himself to us!

Note	Page	
1	51	Columbus: Christopher Columbus, Italian explorer often credited with the discovery of N. America in 1492.
2	51	Galileo: Galileo Galilei, Italian physicist and astronomer persecuted for his belief that the Earth rotated around the sun. He died under house arrest in 1642.
3	51	Wright Brothers: Wilbur and Orville Wright built and flew the first airplane at Kittyhawk, North Carolina in 1904.

Chapter 5

HOW IT WORKS

*R*ARELY HAVE we seen a person fail who has thoroughly followed our path. Those who do not recover are people who cannot or will not completely give themselves to this simple program, usually men and women who are constitutionally incapable of being honest with themselves. There are such unfortunates. They are not at fault; they seem to have been born that way. They are naturally incapable of grasping and developing a manner of living which demands rigorous honesty. Their chances are less than average. There are those, too, who suffer from grave emotional and mental disorders, but many of them do recover if they have the capacity to be honest.

Our stories disclose in a general way what we used to be like, what happened, and what we are like now. If you have decided you want what we have and are willing to go to any length to get it—then you are ready to take certain steps.

At some of these we balked. We thought we could find an easier, softer way. But we could not. With all the earnestness at our command, we beg of you to be fearless and thorough from the very start. Some of us have tried to hold on to our old ideas and the result was nil until we let go absolutely.

Remember that we deal with alcohol-cunning, baffling, powerful! Without help it is too much for us. But there is One who has all power-that One is God. May you find Him now!

Half measures availed us nothing. We stood at the turning point. We asked His protection and care with complete abandon.

Here are the steps we took, which are suggested as a program of recovery:

1. We admitted we were powerless over alcohol-that our lives had become unmanageable.
2. Came to believe that a Power greater than ourselves could restore us to sanity.
3. Made a decision to turn our will and our lives over to the care of God *as we understood Him.*
4. Made a searching and fearless moral inventory of ourselves.
5. Admitted to God, to ourselves, and to another human being the exact nature of our wrongs.
6. Were entirely ready to have God remove all these defects of character.
7. Humbly asked Him to remove our shortcomings.
8. Made a list of all persons we had harmed, and became willing to make amends to them all.
9. Made direct amends to such people wherever possible, except when to do so would injure them or others.
10. Continued to take personal inventory and when we were wrong promptly admitted it.
11. Sought through prayer and meditation to improve our conscious contact with God *as we understood Him,* praying only for knowledge of His will for us and the power to carry that out.

12. Having had a spiritual awakening as the result of these steps, we tried to carry this message to alcoholics, and to practice these principles in all our affairs.

Many of us exclaimed, "What an order! I can't go through with it." Do not be discouraged. No one among us has been able to maintain anything like perfect adherence to these principles. We are not saints. The point is, that we are willing to grow along spiritual lines. The principles we have set down are guides to progress. We claim spiritual progress rather than spiritual perfection.

Our description of the alcoholic, the chapter to the agnostic, and our personal adventures before and after make clear three pertinent ideas:

(a) That we were alcoholic and could not manage our own lives.

(b) That probably no human power could have relieved our alcoholism.

(c) That God could and would if He were sought.

Being convinced, *we were at Step Three*, which is that we decided to turn our will and our life over to God as we understood Him. Just what do we mean by that, and just what do we do?

The first requirement is that we be convinced that any life run on self-will can hardly be a success. On that basis we are almost always in collision with something or somebody, even though our motives are good. Most people try to live by self-propulsion. Each person is like an actor who wants to run the whole show; is forever trying to arrange the lights, the ballet, the scenery and the rest of the players in his own way. If his arrangements would only stay put, if only people would do as he wished, the show would be great. Everybody, including himself, would be pleased. Life would be wonderful. In trying to make these arrangements our actor may sometimes be quite virtuous. He may be kind, considerate, patient, generous; even modest and self-sacrificing. On the other hand, he may be mean, egotistical, selfish and dishonest. But, as with most humans, he is more likely to have varied traits.

What usually happens? The show doesn't come off very well. He begins to think life doesn't treat him right. He decides to exert himself more. He becomes, on the next occasion, still more demanding or gracious, as the case may be. Still the play does not suit him. Admitting he may be somewhat at fault, he is sure that other people are more to blame. He becomes angry, indignant, self-pitying. What is his basic trouble? Is he not really a self-seeker even when trying to be kind? Is he not a victim of the delusion that he can wrest satisfaction and happiness out of this world if he only manages well? Is it not evident to all the rest of the players that these are the things he wants? And do not his actions make each of them wish to retaliate, snatching all they can get out of the show? Is he not, even in his best moments, a producer of confusion rather than harmony?

Our actor is self-centered—ego-centric, as people like to call it nowadays. He is like the retired business man who lolls in the Florida sunshine in the winter complaining of the sad state of the nation; the minister who sighs over the sins of the twentieth century; politicians and reformers who are sure all would be Utopia if the rest of the world would only behave; the outlaw safe cracker who thinks society has wronged him; and the alcoholic who has lost all and is locked up. Whatever our protestations, are not most of us concerned with ourselves, our resentments, or our self-pity?

Selfishness—self-centeredness! That, we think, is the root of our troubles. Driven by a hundred forms of fear, self-delusion, self-seeking, and self-pity, we step on the toes of our fellows and they retaliate. Sometimes they hurt us, seemingly without provocation, but we invariably find that at some time in the past we have made decisions based on self which later placed us in a position to be hurt.

So our troubles, we think, are basically of our own making. They arise out of ourselves, and the alcoholic is an extreme example of self-will run riot, though he usually doesn't think so. Above everything, we alcoholics must be rid of this selfishness. We must, or it kills us! God makes that possible. And there often seems no way of entirely getting rid of self without His aid. Many of us had moral and philosophical convictions galore, but we could not live up to them even though we would have liked to. Neither could we reduce our self-centeredness much by wishing or trying on our own power. We had to have God's help.

This is the how and why of it. First of all, we had to quit playing God. It didn't work. Next, we decided that hereafter in this drama of life, God was going to be our Director. He is the Principal; we are His agents. He is the Father, and we are His children. Most good ideas are simple, and this concept was the keystone of the new and triumphant arch through which we passed to freedom.

When we sincerely took such a position, all sorts of remarkable things followed. We had a new Employer. Being all powerful, He provided what we needed, if we kept close to Him and performed His work well. Established on such a footing we became less and less interested in ourselves, our little plans and designs. More and more we became interested in seeing what we could contribute to life. As we felt new power flow in, as we enjoyed peace of mind, as we discovered we could face life successfully, as we became conscious of His presence, we began to lose our fear of today, tomorrow or the hereafter. We were reborn.

We were now at Step Three. Many of us said to our Maker, *as we understood Him:* "God, I offer myself to Thee-to build with me and to do with me as Thou wilt. Relieve me of the bondage of self, that I may better do Thy will. Take away my difficulties, that victory over them may bear witness to those I would help of Thy Power, Thy Love, and Thy Way of life. May I do Thy will always!" We thought well before taking this step making sure we were ready; that we could at last abandon ourselves utterly to Him.

We found it very desirable to take this spiritual step with an understanding person, such as our wife, best friend or spiritual adviser. But it is better to meet God alone than with one who might misunderstand. The wording was, of course, quite optional so long as we expressed the idea, voicing it without reservation. This was only a beginning, though if honestly and humbly made, an effect, sometimes a very great one, was felt at once.

Next we launched out on a course of vigorous action, the first step of which is a personal housecleaning, which many of us had never attempted. Though our decision was a vital and crucial step, it could have little permanent effect unless at once followed by a strenuous effort to face, and to be rid of, the things in ourselves which had been blocking us. Our liquor was but a symptom. So we had to get down to causes and conditions.

Therefore, we started upon a personal inventory. *This was Step Four.* A business which takes no regular inventory usually goes broke. Taking a commercial inventory is a fact-finding and a fact-facing process. It is an effort to discover the truth about the stock-in-trade. One object is to disclose damaged or unsalable goods, to get rid of them promptly and without regret. If the owner of the business is to be successful, he cannot fool himself about values.

We did exactly the same thing with our lives. We took stock honestly. First, we searched out the flaws in our make-up which caused our failure. Being convinced that self, manifested in various ways, was what had defeated us, we considered its common manifestations.

Resentment is the "number one" offender. It destroys more alcoholics than anything else. From it stem all forms of spiritual disease, for we have been not only mentally and physically ill, we have been spiritually sick. When the spiritual malady is overcome, we straighten out mentally and physically. In dealing with resentments, we set them on paper. We listed people, institutions or principles with whom we were angry. We asked ourselves why we were angry. In most cases it was found that our self-esteem, our pocketbooks, our ambitions, our personal relationships (including sex) were hurt or threatened. So we were sore. We were "burned up."

On our grudge list we set opposite each name our injuries. Was it our self-esteem, our security, our ambitions, our personal, or sex relations, which had been interfered with?

We were usually as definite as this example:

I'm resentful at:	The Cause	Affects my:
Mr. Brown	His attention to my wife.	Sex relations. Self-esteem (fear)
	Told my wife of my mistress.	Sex relations. Self-esteem (fear)
	Brown may get my job at the office.	Security. Self-esteem (fear)
Mrs. Jones	She's a nut - she snubbed me. She committed her husband for drinking. He's my friend. She's a gossip.	Personal relationship. Self-esteem (fear)
My employer	Unreasonable - Unjust - Overbearing - Threatens to fire me for drinking and padding my expense account.	Self-esteem(fear) Security.
My wife	Misunderstands and nags. Likes Brown. Wants house put in her name.	Pride - Personal sex relations - Security (fear)

We went back through our lives. Nothing counted but thoroughness and honesty. When we were finished we considered it carefully. The first thing apparent was that this world and its people were often quite wrong. To conclude that others were wrong was as far as most of us ever got. The usual outcome was that people continued to wrong us and we stayed sore. Sometimes it was remorse and then we were sore at ourselves. But the more we fought and tried to have our own way, the worse matters got. As in war, the victor only *seemed* to win. Our moments of triumph were short-lived.

It is plain that a life which includes deep resentment leads only to futility and unhappiness. To the precise extent that we permit these, do we squander the hours that might have been worth while. But with the alcoholic, whose hope is the maintenance and growth of a spiritual experience, this business of resentment is infinitely grave. We found that it is fatal. For when harboring such feelings we shut ourselves off from the sunlight of the Spirit. The insanity of alcohol returns and we drink again. And with us, to drink is to die.

If we were to live, we had to be free of anger. The grouch and the brainstorm were not for us. They may be the dubious luxury of normal men, but for alcoholics these things are poison.

We turned back to the list, for it held the key to the future. We were prepared to look at it from an entirely different angle. We began to see that the world and its people really dominated us. In that state, the wrong-doing of others, fancied or real, had power to actually kill. How could we escape? We saw that these resentments must be mastered, but how? We could not wish them away any more than alcohol.

This was our course: We realized that the people who wronged us were perhaps spiritually sick.

Though we did not like their symptoms and the way these disturbed us, they, like ourselves, were sick too. We asked God to help us show them the same tolerance, pity, and patience that we would cheerfully grant a sick friend. When a person offended we said to ourselves, "This is a sick man. How can I be helpful to him? God save me from being angry. Thy will be done."

We avoid retaliation or argument. We wouldn't treat sick people that way. If we do, we destroy our chance of being helpful. We cannot be helpful to all people, but at least God will show us how to take a kindly and tolerant view of each and every one.

Referring to our list again. Putting out of our minds the wrongs others had done, we resolutely looked for our own mistakes. Where had we been selfish, dishonest, self-seeking and frightened? Though a situation had not been entirely our fault, we tried to disregard the other person involved entirely. Where were we to blame? The inventory was ours, not the other man's. When we saw our faults we listed them. We placed them before us in black and white. We admitted our wrongs honestly and were willing to set these matters straight.

Notice that the word "fear" is bracketed alongside the difficulties with Mr. Brown, Mrs. Jones, the employer, and the wife. This short word somehow touches about every aspect of our lives. It was an evil and corroding thread; the fabric of our existence was shot through with it. It set in motion trains of circumstances which brought us misfortune we felt we didn't deserve. But did not we, ourselves, set the ball rolling? Sometimes we think fear ought to be classed with stealing. It seems to cause more trouble.

We reviewed our fears thoroughly. We put them on paper, even though we had no resentment in connection with them. We asked ourselves why we had them. Wasn't it because self-reliance failed us? Self-reliance was good as far as it went, but it didn't go far enough. Some of us once had great self-confidence, but it didn't fully solve the fear problem, or any other. When it made us cocky, it was worse.

Perhaps there is a better way—we think so. For we are now on a different basis; the basis of trusting and relying upon God. We trust infinite God rather than our finite selves. We are in the world to play the role He assigns. Just to the extent that we do as we think He would have us, and humbly rely on Him, does He enable us to match calamity with serenity.

We never apologize to anyone for depending upon our Creator. We can laugh at those who think spirituality the way of weakness. Paradoxically, it is the way of strength. The verdict of the ages is that faith means courage. All men of faith have courage. They trust their God. We never apologize for God. Instead we let Him demonstrate, through us, what He can do. We ask Him to remove our fear and direct our attention to what He would have us be. At once, we commence to outgrow fear.

Now about sex. Many of us needed an overhauling there. But above all, we tried to be sensible on this question. It's so easy to get way off the track. Here we find human opinions running to extremes—absurd extremes, perhaps. One set of voices cry that sex is a lust of our lower nature, a base necessity of procreation. Then we have the voices who cry for sex and more sex; who bewail the institution of marriage; who think that most of the troubles of the race are traceable to sex causes. They think we do not have enough of it, or that it isn't the right kind. They see its significance everywhere. One school would allow man no flavor for his fare and the other would have us all on a straight pepper diet. We want to stay out of this controversy. We do not want to be the arbiter of anyone's sex conduct. We all have sex problems. We'd hardly be human if we didn't. What can we do about them?

We reviewed our own conduct over the years past. Where had we been selfish, dishonest, or inconsiderate? Whom had we hurt? Did we unjustifiably arouse jealousy, suspicion or bitterness? Where were we at fault, what should we have done instead? We got this all down on paper and looked at it.

In this way we tried to shape a sane and sound ideal for our future sex life. We subjected each relation to this test— was it selfish or not? We asked God to mold our ideals and help us to live up to them. We remembered always that our sex powers were God-given and therefore good, neither to be used lightly or selfishly nor to be despised and loathed.

Whatever our ideal turns out to be, we must be willing to grow toward it. We must be willing to make amends where we have done harm, provided that we do not bring about still more harm in so doing. In other words, we treat sex as we would any other problem. In meditation, we ask God what we should do about each specific matter. The right answer will come, if we want it.

God alone can judge our sex situation. Counsel with

persons is often desirable, but we let God be the final judge. We realize that some people are as fanatical about sex as others are loose. We avoid hysterical thinking or advice.

Suppose we fall short of the chosen ideal and stumble? Does this mean we are going to get drunk? Some people tell us so. But this is only a half-truth. It depends on us and on our motives. If we are sorry for what we have done, and have the honest desire to let God take us to better things, we believe we will be forgiven and will have learned our lesson. If we are not sorry, and our conduct continues to harm others, we are quite sure to drink. We are not theorizing. These are facts out of our experience.

To sum up about sex: We earnestly pray for the right ideal, for guidance in each questionable situation, for sanity, and for the strength to do the right thing. If sex is very troublesome, we throw ourselves the harder into helping others. We think of their needs and work for them. This takes us out of ourselves. It quiets the imperious urge, when to yield would mean heartache.

If we have been thorough about our personal inventory, we have written down a lot. We have listed and analyzed our resentments. We have begun to comprehend their futility and their fatality. We have commenced to see their terrible destructiveness. We have begun to learn tolerance, patience and good will toward all men, even our enemies, for we look on them as sick people. We have listed the people we have hurt by our conduct, and are willing to straighten out the past if we can.

In this book you read again and again that faith did

for us what we could not do for ourselves. We hope you are convinced now that God can remove whatever self-will has blocked you off from Him. If you have already made a decision, and an inventory of your grosser handicaps, you have made a good beginning. That being so you have swallowed and digested some big chunks of truth about yourself.

Chapter 6

INTO ACTION

*H*AVING MADE our personal inventory, what shall we do about it? We have been trying to get a new attitude, a new relationship with our Creator, and to discover the obstacles in our path. We have admitted certain defects; we have ascertained in a rough way what the trouble is; we have put our finger on the weak items in our personal inventory. Now these are about to be cast out. This requires action on our part, which, when completed, will mean that we have admitted to God, to ourselves, and to another human being, the exact nature of our defects. This brings us to *the Fifth Step* in the program of recovery mentioned in the preceding chapter.

This is perhaps difficult—especially discussing our defects with another person. We think we have done well enough in admitting these things to ourselves. There is doubt about that. In actual practice, we usually find a solitary self-appraisal insufficient. Many of us thought it necessary to go much further. We will be more reconciled to discussing ourselves with another person when we see good reasons why we should do so. The best reason first: If we skip this vital step, we may not overcome drinking. Time after time newcomers have tried to keep to themselves certain facts about their lives. Trying to avoid this humbling experience, they have turned to easier methods. Almost invariably they got drunk. Having persevered with the rest of the program, they wondered why they fell. We think the reason is that they never completed their house-cleaning. They took inventory all right, but hung on to some of the worst items in stock. They only *thought* they had lost their egoism and fear; they only *thought* they had humbled themselves. But they had not learned enough of humility, fearlessness and honesty, in the sense we find it necessary, until they told someone else *all* their life story.

More than most people, the alcoholic leads a double life. He is very much the actor. To the outer world he presents his stage character. This is the one he likes his fellows to see. He wants to enjoy a certain reputation, but knows in his heart he doesn't deserve it.

The inconsistency is made worse by the things he does on his sprees. Coming to his senses, he is revolted at certain episodes he vaguely remembers. These memories are a nightmare. He trembles to think someone might have observed him. As fast as he can, he pushes these memories far inside himself. He hopes they will never see the light of day. He is under constant fear and tension—that makes for more drinking.

Psychologists are inclined to agree with us. We have spent thousands of dollars for examinations. We know but few instances where we have given these doctors a fair break. We have seldom told them the whole truth nor have we followed their advice. Unwilling to be honest with these sympathetic men, we were honest with no one else. Small wonder many in the medical profession have a low opinion of alcoholics and their chance for recovery!

We must be entirely honest with somebody if we

expect to live long or happily in this world. Rightly and naturally, we think well before we choose the person or persons with whom to take this intimate and confidential step. Those of us belonging to a religious denomination which requires confession must, and of course, will want to go to the properly appointed authority whose duty it is to receive it. Though we have no religious connection, we may still do well to talk with someone ordained by an established religion. We often find such a person quick to see and understand our problem. Of course, we sometimes encounter people who do not understand alcoholics.

If we cannot or would rather not do this, we search our acquaintance for a close-mouthed, understanding friend. Perhaps our doctor or psychologist will be the person. It may be one of our own family, but we cannot disclose anything to our wives or our parents which will hurt them and make them unhappy. We have no right to save our own skin at another person's expense. Such parts of our story we tell to someone who will understand, yet be unaffected. The rule is we must be hard on ourself, but always considerate of others.

Notwithstanding the great necessity for discussing ourselves with someone, it may be one is so situated that there is no suitable person available. If that is so, this step may be postponed, only, however, if we hold ourselves in complete readiness to go through with it at the first opportunity. We say this because we are very anxious that we talk to the right person. It is important that he be able to keep a confidence; that he fully understand and approve what we are driving at;

that he will not try to change our plan. But we must not use this as a mere excuse to postpone.

When we decide who is to hear our story, we waste no time. We have a written inventory and we are prepared for a long talk. We explain to our partner what we are about to do and why we have to do it. He should realize that we are engaged upon a life-and-death errand. Most people approached in this way will be glad to help; they will be honored by our confidence.

We pocket our pride and go to it, illuminating every twist of character, every dark cranny of the past. Once we have taken this step, withholding nothing, we are delighted. We can look the world in the eye. We can be alone at perfect peace and ease. Our fears fall from us. We begin to feel the nearness of our Creator. We may have had certain spiritual beliefs, but now we begin to have a spiritual experience. The feeling that the drink problem has disappeared will often come strongly. We feel we are on the Broad Highway, walking hand in hand with the Spirit of the Universe.

Returning home we find a place where we can be quiet for an hour, carefully reviewing what we have done. We thank God from the bottom of our heart that we know Him better. Taking this book down from our shelf we turn to the page which contains the twelve steps. Carefully reading the first five proposals we ask if we have omitted anything, for we are building an arch through which we shall walk a free man at last. Is our work solid so far? Are the stones properly in place? Have we skimped on the cement put into the foundation? Have we tried to make mortar without sand?

If we can answer to our satisfaction, we then look at *Step Six.* We have emphasized willingness as being indispensable. Are we now ready to let God remove from us all the things which we have admitted are objectionable? Can He now take them all—every one? If we still cling to something we will not let go, we ask God to help us be willing.

When ready, we say something like this: "My Creator, I am now willing that you should have all of me, good and bad. I pray that you now remove from me every single defect of character which stands in the way of my usefulness to you and my fellows. Grant me strength, as I go out from here, to do your bidding. Amen." We have then completed *Step Seven.*

Now we need more action, without which we find that "Faith without works is dead." Let's look at *Steps Eight and Nine.* We have a list of all persons we have harmed and to whom we are willing to make amends. We made it when we took inventory. We subjected ourselves to a drastic self-appraisal. Now we go out to our fellows and repair the damage done in the past. We attempt to sweep away the debris which has accumulated out of our effort to live on self-will and run the show ourselves. If we haven't the will to do this, we ask until it comes. Remember it was agreed at the beginning *we would go to any lengths for victory over alcohol.*

Probably there are still some misgivings. As we look over the list of business acquaintances and friends we have hurt, we may feel diffident about going to some of them on a spiritual basis. Let us be reassured. To some people we need not, and probably should not emphasize the spiritual feature on our first approach.

We might prejudice them. At the moment we are trying to put our lives in order. But this is not an end in itself. Our real purpose is to fit ourselves to be of maximum service to God and the people about us. It is seldom wise to approach an individual, who still smarts from our injustice to him, and announce that we have gone religious. In the prize ring, this would be called leading with the chin. Why lay ourselves open to being branded fanatics or religious bores? We may kill a future opportunity to carry a beneficial message. But our man is sure to be impressed with a sincere desire to set right the wrong. He is going to be more interested in a demonstration of good will than in our talk of spiritual discoveries.

We don't use this as an excuse for shying away from the subject of God. When it will serve any good purpose, we are willing to announce our convictions with tact and common sense. The question of how to approach the man we hated will arise. It may be he has done us more harm than we have done him and, though we may have acquired a better attitude toward him, we are still not too keen about admitting our faults. Nevertheless, with a person we dislike, we take the bit in our teeth. It is harder to go to an enemy than to a friend, but we find it much more beneficial to us. We go to him in a helpful and forgiving spirit, confessing our former ill feeling and expressing our regret.

Under no condition do we criticize such a person or argue. Simply we tell him that we will never get over drinking until we have done our utmost to straighten out the past. We are there to sweep off our side of the street, realizing that nothing worth while can be accomplished until we do so, never trying to tell him what he should do. His faults are not discussed. We stick to our own. If our manner is calm, frank, and open, we will be gratified with the result.

In nine cases out of ten the unexpected happens. Sometimes the man we are calling upon admits his own fault, so feuds of years' standing melt away in an hour. Rarely do we fail to make satisfactory progress. Our former enemies sometimes praise what we are doing and wish us well. Occasionally, they will offer assistance. It should not matter, however, if someone does throw us out of his office. We have made our demonstration, done our part. It's water over the dam.

Most alcoholics owe money. We do not dodge our creditors. Telling them what we are trying to do, we make no bones about our drinking; they usually know it anyway, whether we think so or not. Nor are we afraid of disclosing our alcoholism on the theory it may cause financial harm. Approached in this way, the most ruthless creditor will sometimes surprise us. Arranging the best deal we can we let these people know we are sorry. Our drinking has made us slow to pay. We must lose our fear of creditors no matter how far we have to go, for we are liable to drink if we are afraid to face them.

Perhaps we have committed a criminal offense which might land us in jail if it were known to the authorities. We may be short in our accounts and unable to make good. We have already admitted this in confidence to another person, but we are sure we would be imprisoned or lose our job if it were known. Maybe it's only a petty offense such as padding the expense account. Most of us have done that sort of thing.

Maybe we are divorced, and have remarried but haven't kept up the alimony to number one. She is indignant about it, and has a warrant out for our arrest. That's a common form of trouble too.

Although these reparations take innumerable forms, there are some general principles which we find guiding. Reminding ourselves that we have decided to go to any lengths to find a spiritual experience, we ask that we be given strength and direction to do the right thing, no matter what the personal consequences may be. We may lose our position or reputation or face jail, but we are willing. We have to be. We must not shrink at anything.

Usually, however, other people are involved. Therefore, we are not to be the hasty and foolish martyr who would needlessly sacrifice others to save himself from the alcoholic pit. A man we know had remarried. Because of resentment and drinking, he had not paid alimony to his first wife. She was furious. She went to court and got an order for his arrest. He had commenced our way of life, had secured a position, and was getting his head above water. It would have been impressive heroics if he had walked up to the Judge and said, "Here I am."

We thought he ought to be willing to do that if necessary, but if he were in jail he could provide nothing for either family. We suggested he write his first wife admitting his faults and asking forgiveness. He did, and also sent a small amount of money. He told her what he would try to do in the future. He said he was perfectly willing to go to jail if she insisted. Of course she did not, and the whole situation has long since been adjusted.

Before taking drastic action which might implicate other people we secure their consent. If we have obtained permission, have consulted with others, asked God to help and the drastic step is indicated we must not shrink.

This brings to mind a story about one of our friends. While drinking, he accepted a sum of money from a bitterly-hated business rival, giving him no receipt for it. He subsequently denied having received the money and used the incident as a basis for discrediting the man. He thus used his own wrong-doing as a means of destroying the reputation of another. In fact, his rival was ruined.

He felt that he had done a wrong he could not possibly make right. If he opened that old affair, he was afraid it would destroy the reputation of his partner, disgrace his family and take away his means of livelihood. What right had he to involve those dependent upon him? How could he possibly make a public statement exonerating his rival?

After consulting with his wife and partner he came to the conclusion that is was better to take those risks than to stand before his Creator guilty of such ruinous slander. He saw that he had to place the outcome in God's hands or he would soon start drinking again, and all would be lost anyhow. He attended church for the first time in many years. After the sermon, he quietly got up and made an explanation. His action met widespread approval, and today he is one of the most trusted citizens of his town. This all happened years ago.

The chances are that we have domestic troubles. Perhaps we are mixed up with women in a fashion we wouldn't care to have advertised. We doubt if, in this respect, alcoholics are fundamentally much worse than other people. But drinking does complicate sex relations in the home. After a few years with an alcoholic, a wife gets worn out, resentful and uncommunicative. How could she be anything else? The husband begins to feel lonely, sorry for himself. He commences to look around in the night clubs, or their equivalent, for something besides liquor. Perhaps he is having a secret and exciting affair with "the girl who understands." In fairness we must say that she may understand, but what are we going to do about a thing like that? A man so involved often feels very remorseful at times, especially if he is married to a loyal and courageous girl who has literally gone through hell for him.

Whatever the situation, we usually have to do something about it. If we are sure our wife does not know, should we tell her? Not always, we think. If she knows in a general way that we have been wild, should we tell her in detail? Undoubtedly we should admit our fault. She may insist on knowing all the particulars. She will want to know who the woman is and where she is. We feel we ought to say to her that we have no right to involve another person. We are sorry for what we have done and, God willing, it shall not be repeated. More than that we cannot do; we have no right to go further. Though there may be justifiable exceptions, and though we wish to lay down no rule of any sort, we have often found this the best course to take.

Our design for living is not a one-way street. It is as good for the wife as for the husband. If we can

forget, so can she. It is better, however, that one does
not needlessly name a person upon whom she can vent
jealousy.

Perhaps there are some cases where the utmost frank-
ness is demanded. No outsider can appraise such an
intimate situation. It may be that both will decide that
the way of good sense and loving kindness is to let by-
gones be by-gones. Each might pray about it, having
the other one's happiness uppermost in mind. Keep it
always in sight that we are dealing with that most terrible human emotion-jealousy. Good generalship may
decide that the problem be attacked on the flank rather
than risk a face-to-face combat.

If we have no such complication, there is plenty we
should do at home. Sometimes we hear an alcoholic
say that the only thing he needs to do is to keep sober.
Certainly he must keep sober, for there will be no home
if he doesn't. But he is yet a long way from making
good to the wife or parents whom for years he has so
shockingly treated. Passing all understanding is the
patience mothers and wives have had with alcoholics.
Had this not been so, many of us would have no homes
today, would perhaps be dead.

The alcoholic is like a tornado roaring his way
through the lives of others. Hearts are broken. Sweet
relationships are dead. Affections have been uprooted.
Selfish and inconsiderate habits have kept the home in
turmoil. We feel a man is unthinking when he says
that sobriety is enough. He is like the farmer who came
up out of his cyclone cellar to find his home ruined.
To his wife, he remarked, "Don't see anything the matter here, Ma. Ain't it grand the wind stopped blowin'?"

Yes, there is a long period of reconstruction ahead. We must take the lead. A remorseful mumbling that we are sorry won't fill the bill at all. We ought to sit down with the family and frankly analyze the past as we now see it, being very careful not to criticize them. Their defects may be glaring, but the chances are that our own actions are partly responsible. So we clean house with the family, asking each morning in meditation that our Creator show us the way of patience, tolerance, kindliness and love.

The spiritual life is not a theory. *We have to live it.* Unless one's family expresses a desire to live upon spiritual principles we think we ought not to urge them. We should not talk incessantly to them about spiritual matters. They will change in time. Our behavior will convince them more than our words. We must remember that ten or twenty years of drunkenness would make a skeptic out of anyone.

There may be some wrongs we can never fully right. We don't worry about them if we can honestly say to ourselves that we would right them if we could. Some people cannot be seen—we send them an honest letter. And there may be a valid reason for postponement in some cases. But we don't delay if it can be avoided. We should be sensible, tactful, considerate and humble without being servile or scraping. As God's people we stand on our feet; we don't crawl before anyone.

If we are painstaking about this phase of our development, we will be amazed before we are half way through. We are going to know a new freedom and a new happiness. We will not regret the past nor wish to shut the door on it. We will comprehend the word serenity and we will know peace. No matter how far down the scale we have gone, we will see how our experience can benefit others. That feeling of uselessness and self-pity will disappear. We will lose interest in selfish things and gain interest in our fellows. Self-seeking will slip away. Our whole attitude and outlook upon life will change. Fear of people and of economic insecurity will leave us. We will intuitively know how to handle situations which used to baffle us. We will suddenly realize that God is doing for us what we could not do for ourselves.

Are these extravagant promises? We think not. They are being fulfilled among us—sometimes quickly, sometimes slowly. They will always materialize if we work for them.

This thought brings us to *Step Ten*, which suggests we continue to take personal inventory and continue to set right any new mistakes as we go along. We vigorously commenced this way of living as we cleaned up the past. We have entered the world of the Spirit. Our next function is to grow in understanding and effectiveness. This is not an overnight matter. It should continue for our lifetime. Continue to watch for selfishness, dishonesty, resentment, and fear. When these crop up, we ask God at once to remove them. We discuss them with someone immediately and make amends quickly if we have harmed anyone. Then we resolutely turn our thoughts to someone we can help. Love and tolerance of others is our code.

And we have ceased fighting anything or anyone— even alcohol. For by this time sanity will have returned. We will seldom be interested in liquor. If tempted, we recoil from it as from a hot flame. We react sanely and normally, and we will find that this has happened automatically. We will see that our new attitude toward liquor has been given us without any thought or effort on our part. It just comes! That is the miracle of it. We are not fighting it, neither are we avoiding temptation. We feel as though we had been placed in a position of neutrality—safe and protected. We have not even sworn off. Instead, the problem has been removed. It does not exist for us. We are neither cocky nor are we afraid. That is our experience. That is how we react so long as we keep in fit spiritual condition.

It is easy to let up on the spiritual program of action and rest on our laurels. We are headed for trouble if we do, for alcohol is a subtle foe. We are not cured of alcoholism. What we really have is a daily reprieve contingent on the maintenance of our spiritual condition. Every day is a day when we must carry the vision of God's will into all of our activities. "How can I best serve Thee—Thy will (not mine) be done." These are thoughts which must go with us constantly. We can exercise our will power along this line all we wish. It is the proper use of the will.

Much has already been said about receiving strength, inspiration, and direction from Him who has all knowledge and power. If we have carefully followed directions, we have begun to sense the flow of His Spirit into us. To some extent we have become God-conscious. We have begun to develop this vital sixth sense. But we must go further and that means more action.

Step Eleven suggests prayer and meditation. We shouldn't be shy on this matter of prayer. Better men than we are using it constantly. It works, if we have the proper attitude and work at it. It would be easy to be vague about this matter. Yet, we believe we can make some definite and valuable suggestions.

When we retire at night, we constructively review our day. Were we resentful, selfish, dishonest or afraid? Do we owe an apology? Have we kept something to ourselves which should be discussed with another person at once? Were we kind and loving toward all? What could we have done better? Were we thinking of ourselves most of the time? Or were we thinking of what we could do for others, of what we could pack into the stream of life? But we must be careful not to drift into worry, remorse or morbid reflection, for that would diminish our usefulness to others. After making our review we ask God's forgiveness and inquire what corrective measures should be taken.

On awakening let us think about the twenty-four hours ahead. We consider our plans for the day. Before we begin, we ask God to direct our thinking, especially asking that it be divorced from self-pity, dishonest or self-seeking motives. Under these conditions we can employ our mental faculties with assurance, for after all God gave us brains to use. Our thought-life will be placed on a much higher plane when our thinking is cleared of wrong motives.

In thinking about our day we may face indecision. We may not be able to determine which course to take. Here we ask God for inspiration, an intuitive thought or a decision. We relax and take it easy. We don't struggle. We are often surprised how the right answers come after we have tried this for a while.

What used to be the hunch or the occasional inspiration gradually becomes a working part of the mind. Being still inexperienced and having just made conscious contact with God, it is not probable that we are going to be inspired at all times. We might pay for this presumption in all sorts of absurd actions and ideas. Nevertheless, we find that our thinking will, as time passes, be more and more on the plane of inspiration. We come to rely upon it.

We usually conclude the period of meditation with a prayer that we be shown all through the day what our next step is to be, that we be given whatever we need to take care of such problems. We ask especially for freedom from self-will, and are careful to make no request for ourselves only. We may ask for ourselves, however, if others will be helped. We are careful never to pray for our own selfish ends. Many of us have wasted a lot of time doing that and it doesn't work. You can easily see why.

If circumstances warrant, we ask our wives or friends to join us in morning meditation. If we belong to a religious denomination which requires a definite morning devotion, we attend to that also. If not members of religious bodies, we sometimes select and memorize a few set prayers which emphasize the principles we have been discussing. There are many helpful books also. Suggestions about these may be obtained from one's priest, minister, or rabbi. Be quick to see where religious people are right. Make use of what they offer.

As we go through the day we pause, when agitated or doubtful, and ask for the right thought or action. We constantly remind ourselves we are no longer running the show, humbly saying to ourselves many times each day "Thy will be done." We are then in much less danger of excitement, fear, anger, worry, self-pity, or foolish decisions. We become much more efficient. We do not tire so easily, for we are not burning up energy foolishly as we did when we were trying to arrange life to suit ourselves.

It works—it really does.

We alcoholics are undisciplined. So we let God discipline us in the simple way we have just outlined.

But this is not all. There is action and more action. "Faith without works is dead." The next chapter is entirely devoted to *Step Twelve*.

Chapter 7

WORKING WITH OTHERS

$\mathcal{P}$RACTICAL EXPERIENCE shows that nothing will so much insure immunity from drinking as intensive work with other alcoholics. It works when other activities fail. This is our *twelfth suggestion*: Carry this message to other alcoholics! You can help when no one else can. You can secure their confidence when others fail. Remember they are very ill.

Life will take on new meaning. To watch people recover, to see them help others, to watch loneliness vanish, to see a fellowship grow up about you, to have a host of friends—this is an experience you must not miss. We know you will not want to miss it. Frequent contact with newcomers and with each other is the bright spot of our lives.

Perhaps you are not acquainted with any drinkers who want to recover. You can easily find some by asking a few doctors, ministers, priests or hospitals. They will be only too glad to assist you. Don't start out as an evangelist or reformer. Unfortunately a lot of prejudice exists. You will be handicapped if you arouse it. Ministers and doctors are competent and you can learn much from them if you wish, but it happens that because of your own drinking experience you can be uniquely useful to other alcoholics. So cooperate; never criticize. To be helpful is our only aim.

When you discover a prospect for Alcoholics Anonymous, find out all you can about him. If he does not want to stop drinking, don't waste time trying to persuade him. You may spoil a later opportunity. This advice is given for his family also. They should be patient, realizing they are dealing with a sick person.

If there is any indication that he wants to stop, have a good talk with the person most interested in him— usually his wife. Get an idea of his behavior, his problems, his background, the seriousness of his condition, and his religious leanings. You need this information to put yourself in his place, to see how you would like him to approach you if the tables were turned.

Sometimes it is wise to wait till he goes on a binge. The family may object to this, but unless he is in a dangerous physical condition, it is better to risk it. Don't deal with him when he is very drunk, unless he is ugly and the family needs your help. Wait for the end of the spree, or at least for a lucid interval. Then let his family or a friend ask him if he wants to quit for good and if he would go to any extreme to do so. If he says yes, then his attention should be drawn to you as a person who has recovered. You should be described to him as one of a fellowship who, as part of their own recovery, try to help others and who will be glad to talk to him if he cares to see you.

If he does not want to see you, never force yourself upon him. Neither should the family hysterically plead with him to do anything, nor should they tell him much about you. They should wait for the end of his next drinking bout. You might place this book where he can see it in the interval. Here no specific rule can be given. The family must decide these things. But urge them not to be over-anxious, for that might spoil matters.

Usually the family should not try to tell your story. When possible, avoid meeting a man through his family. Approach through a doctor or an institution is a better bet. If your man needs hospitalization, he should have it, but not forcibly unless he is violent. Let the doctor, if he will, tell him he has something in the way of a solution.

When your man is better, the doctor might suggest a visit from you. Though you have talked with the family, leave them out of the first discussion. Under these conditions your prospect will see he is under no pressure. He will feel he can deal with you without being nagged by his family. Call on him while he is still jittery. He may be more receptive when depressed.

See your man alone, if possible. At first engage in general conversation. After a while, turn the talk to some phase of drinking. Tell him enough about your drinking habits, symptoms, and experiences to encourage him to speak of himself. If he wishes to talk, let him do so. You will thus get a better idea of how you ought to proceed. If he is not communicative, give him a sketch of your drinking career up to the time you quit. But say nothing, for the moment, of how that was accomplished. If he is in a serious mood dwell on the troubles liquor has caused you, being careful not to moralize or lecture. If his mood is light, tell him humorous stories of your escapades. Get him to tell some of his.

When he sees you know all about the drinking game, commence to describe yourself as an alcoholic.

Tell him how baffled you were, how you finally learned that you were sick. Give him an account of the struggles you made to stop. Show him the mental twist which leads to the first drink of a spree. We suggest you do this as we have done it in the chapter on alcoholism. If he is alcoholic, he will understand you at once. He will match your mental inconsistencies with some of his own.

If you are satisfied that he is a real alcoholic, begin to dwell on the hopeless feature of the malady. Show him, from your own experience, how the queer mental condition surrounding that first drink prevents normal functioning of the will power. Don't, at this stage, refer to this book, unless he has seen it and wishes to discuss it. And be careful not to brand him as an alcoholic. Let him draw his own conclusion. If he sticks to the idea that he can still control his drinking, tell him that possibly he can—if he is not too alcoholic. But insist that if he is severely afflicted, there may be little chance he can recover by himself.

Continue to speak of alcoholism as an illness, a fatal malady. Talk about the conditions of body and mind which accompany it. Keep his attention focused mainly on your personal experience. Explain that many are doomed who never realize their predicament. Doctors are rightly loath to tell alcoholic patients the whole story unless it will serve some good purpose. But you may talk to him about the hopelessness of alcoholism because you offer a solution. You will soon have your friend admitting he has many, if not all, of the traits of the alcoholic. If his own doctor is willing to tell him that he is alcoholic, so much the better. Even though your protégé may not have entirely admitted his condition, he has become very curious to know how you got well. Let him ask you that question, if he will. *Tell him exactly what happened to you*. Stress the spiritual feature freely. If the man be agnostic or atheist, make it emphatic that *he does not have to agree with your conception of God*. He can choose any conception he likes, provided it makes sense to him. *The main thing is that he be willing to believe in a Power greater than himself and that he live by spiritual principles.*

When dealing with such a person, you had better use everyday language to describe spiritual principles. There is no use arousing any prejudice he may have against certain theological terms and conceptions about which he may already be confused. Don't raise such issues, no matter what your own convictions are.

Your prospect may belong to a religious denomination. His religious education and training may be far superior to yours. In that case he is going to wonder how you can add anything to what he already knows. But he will be curious to learn why his own convictions have not worked and why yours seem to work so well. He may be an example of the truth that faith alone is insufficient. To be vital, faith must be accompanied by self sacrifice and unselfish, constructive action. Let him see that you are not there to instruct him in religion. Admit that he probably knows more about it than you do, but call to his attention the fact that however deep his faith and knowledge, he could not have applied it or he would not drink. Perhaps your story will help him see where he has failed to practice the very precepts he knows so well. We represent no

particular faith or denomination. We are dealing only
with general principles common to most denominations.

Outline the program of action, explaining how you
made a self-appraisal, how you straightened out your
past and why you are now endeavoring to be helpful to
him. It is important for him to realize that your attempt to pass this on to him plays a vital part in your
own recovery. Actually, he may be helping you more
than you are helping him. Make it plain he is under no
obligation to you, that you hope only that he will try to
help other alcoholics when he escapes his own difficulties. Suggest how important it is that he place the
welfare of other people ahead of his own. Make it clear
that he is not under pressure, that he needn't see you
again if he doesn't want to. You should not be offended
if he wants to call it off, for he has helped you more
than you have helped him. If your talk has been sane,
quiet and full of human understanding, you have perhaps made a friend. Maybe you have disturbed him
about the question of alcoholism. This is all to the
good. The more hopeless he feels, the better. He will
be more likely to follow your suggestions.

Your candidate may give reasons why he need not
follow all of the program. He may rebel at the thought
of a drastic housecleaning which requires discussion
with other people. Do not contradict such views. Tell
him you once felt as he does, but you doubt whether
you would have made much progress had you not taken
action. On your first visit tell him about the Fellowship of Alcoholics Anonymous. If he shows interest,
lend him your copy of this book.

Unless your friend wants to talk further about himself, do not wear out your welcome. Give him a chance to think it over. If you do stay, let him steer the conversation in any direction he likes. Sometimes a new man is anxious to proceed at once. And you may be tempted to let him do so. This is sometimes a mistake. If he has trouble later, he is likely to say you rushed him. You will be most successful with alcoholics if you do not exhibit any passion for crusade or reform. Never talk down to an alcoholic from any moral or spiritual hilltop; simply lay out the kit of spiritual tools for his inspection. Show him how they worked with you. Offer him friendship and fellowship. Tell him that if he wants to get well you will do anything to help.

If he is not interested in your solution, if he expects you to act only as a banker for his financial difficulties or a nurse for his sprees, you may have to drop him until he changes his mind. This he may do after he gets hurt some more.

If he is sincerely interested and wants to see you again, ask him to read this book in the interval. After doing that, he must decide for himself whether he wants to go on. He should not be pushed or prodded by you, his wife, or his friends. If he is to find God, the desire must come from within.

If he thinks he can do the job in some other way, or prefers some other spiritual approach, encourage him to follow his own conscience. We have no monopoly on God; we merely have an approach that worked with us. But point out that we alcoholics have much in common and that you would like, in any case, to be friendly. Let it go at that.

Do not be discouraged if your prospect does not respond at once. Search out another alcoholic and try again. You are sure to find someone desperate enough to accept with eagerness what you offer. We find it a waste of time to keep chasing a man who cannot or will not work with you. If you leave such a person alone, he may soon become convinced that he cannot recover by himself. To spend too much time on any one situation is to deny some other alcoholic an opportunity to live and be happy. One of our Fellowship failed entirely with his first half dozen prospects. He often says that if he had continued to work on them, he might have deprived many others, who have since recovered, of their chance.

Suppose now you are making your second visit to a man. He has read this volume and says he is prepared to go through with the Twelve Steps of the program of recovery. Having had the experience yourself, you can give him much practical advice. Let him know you are available if he wishes to make a decision and tell his story, but do not insist upon it if he prefers to consult someone else.

He may be broke and homeless. If he is, you might try to help him about getting a job, or give him a little financial assistance. But you should not deprive your family or creditors of money they should have. Perhaps you will want to take the man into your home for a few days. But be sure you use discretion. Be certain he will be welcomed by your family, and that he is not trying to impose upon you for money, connections, or shelter. Permit that and you only harm him. You will be making it possible for him to be insincere.

You may be aiding in his destruction rather than his recovery.

Never avoid these responsibilities, but be sure you are doing the right thing if you assume them. Helping others is the foundation stone of your recovery. A kindly act once in a while isn't enough. You have to act the Good Samaritan every day, if need be. It may mean the loss of many nights' sleep, great interference with your pleasures, interruptions to your business. It may mean sharing your money and your home, counseling frantic wives and relatives, innumerable trips to police courts, sanitariums, hospitals, jails and asylums. Your telephone may jangle at any time of the day or night. Your wife may sometimes say she is neglected. A drunk may smash the furniture in your home, or burn a mattress. You may have to fight with him if he is violent. Sometimes you will have to call a doctor and administer sedatives under his direction. Another time you may have to send for the police or an ambulance. Occasionally you will have to meet such conditions.

We seldom allow an alcoholic to live in our homes for long at a time. It is not good for him, and it sometimes creates serious complications in a family.

Though an alcoholic does not respond, there is no reason why you should neglect his family. You should continue to be friendly to them. The family should be offered your way of life. Should they accept and practice spiritual principles, there is a much better chance that the head of the family will recover. And even though he continues to drink, the family will find life more bearable.

For the type of alcoholic who is able and willing to

get well, little charity, in the ordinary sense of the word, is needed or wanted. The men who cry for money and shelter before conquering alcohol, are on the wrong track. Yet we do go to great extremes to provide each other with these very things, when such action is warranted. This may seem inconsistent, but we think it is not.

It is not the matter of giving that is in question, but when and how to give. That often makes the difference between failure and success. The minute we put our work on a service plane, the alcoholic commences to rely upon our assistance rather than upon God. He clamors for this or that, claiming he cannot master alcohol until his material needs are cared for. Nonsense. Some of us have taken very hard knocks to learn this truth: Job or no job—wife or no wife—we simply do not stop drinking so long as we place dependence upon other people ahead of dependence on God.

Burn the idea into the consciousness of every man that he can get well regardless of anyone. The only condition is that he trust in God and clean house.

Now, the domestic problem: There may be divorce, separation, or just strained relations. When your prospect has made such reparation as he can to his family, and has thoroughly explained to them the new principles by which he is living, he should proceed to put those principles into action at home. That is, if he is lucky enough to have a home. Though his family be at fault in many respects, he should not be concerned about that. He should concentrate on his own spiritual demonstration. Argument and fault-finding are to be avoided like the plague. In many homes this is a difficult thing to do, but it must be done if any results are to be expected. If persisted in for a few months, the effect on a man's family is sure to be great. The most incompatible people discover they have a basis upon which they can meet. Little by little the family may see their own defects and admit them. These can then be discussed in an atmosphere of helpfulness and friendliness.

After they have seen tangible results, the family will perhaps want to go along. These things will come to pass naturally and in good time provided, however, the alcoholic continues to demonstrate that he can be sober, considerate, and helpful, regardless of what anyone says or does. Of course, we all fall much below this standard many times. But we must try to repair the damage immediately lest we pay the penalty by a spree.

If there be divorce or separation, there should be no undue haste for the couple to get together. The man should be sure of his recovery. The wife should fully understand his new way of life. If their old relationship is to be resumed it must be on a better basis, since the former did not work. This means a new attitude and spirit all around. Sometimes it is to the best interest of all concerned that a couple remain apart. Obviously, no rule can be laid down. Let the alcoholic continue his program day by day. When the time for living together has come, it will be apparent to both parties.

Let no alcoholic say he cannot recover unless he has his family back. This just isn't so. In some cases the wife will never come back for one reason or another. Remind the prospect that his recovery is not dependent upon people. It is dependent upon his relationship with God. We have seen men get well whose families have not returned at all. We have seen others slip when the family came back too soon.

Both you and the new man must walk day by day in the path of spiritual progress. If you persist, remarkable things will happen. When we look back, we realize that the things which came to us when we put ourselves in God's hands were better than anything we could have planned. Follow the dictates of a Higher Power and you will presently live in a new and wonderful world, no matter what your present circumstances!

When working with a man and his family, you should take care not to participate in their quarrels. You may spoil your chance of being helpful if you do. But urge upon a man's family that he has been a very sick person and should be treated accordingly. You should warn against arousing resentment or jealousy. You should point out that his defects of character are not going to disappear over night. Show them that he has entered upon a period of growth. Ask them to remember, when they are impatient, the blessed fact of his sobriety.

If you have been successful in solving your own domestic problems, tell the newcomer's family how that was accomplished. In this way you can set them on the right track without becoming critical of them. The story of how you and your wife settled your difficulties is worth any amount of criticism.

Assuming we are spiritually fit, we can do all sorts of things alcoholics are not supposed to do. People have said we must not go where liquor is served; we must not have it in our homes; we must shun friends who drink; we must avoid moving pictures which show drinking scenes; we must not go into bars; our friends must hide their bottles if we go to their houses; we mustn't think or be reminded about alcohol at all. Our experience shows that this is not necessarily so.

We meet these conditions every day. An alcoholic who cannot meet them, still has an alcoholic mind; there is something the matter with his spiritual status. His only chance for sobriety would be some place like the Greenland Ice Cap, and even there an Eskimo might turn up with a bottle of scotch and ruin everything! Ask any woman who has sent her husband to distant places on the theory he would escape the alcohol problem.

In our belief any scheme of combating alcoholism which proposes to shield the sick man from temptation is doomed to failure. If the alcoholic tries to shield himself he may succeed for a time, but he usually winds up with a bigger explosion than ever. We have tried these methods. These attempts to do the impossible have always failed.

So our rule is not to avoid a place where there is drinking, *if we have a legitimate reason for being there*. That includes bars, nightclubs, dances, receptions, weddings, even plain ordinary whoopee parties. To a person who has had experience with an alcoholic, this may seem like tempting Providence, but it isn't.

You will note that we made an important qualification. Therefore, ask yourself on each occasion, "Have I any good social, business, or personal reason for going to this place? Or am I expecting to steal a little vicarious pleasure from the atmosphere of such places?" If you answer these questions satisfactorily, you need have no apprehension. Go or stay away, whichever seems best. But be sure you are on solid spiritual ground before you start and that your motive in going is thoroughly good. Do not think of what you will get out of the occasion. Think of what you can bring to it. But if you are shaky, you had better work with another alcoholic instead!

Why sit with a long face in places where there is drinking, sighing about the good old days. If it is a happy occasion, try to increase the pleasure of those there; if a business occasion, go and attend to your business enthusiastically. If you are with a person who wants to eat in a bar, by all means go along. Let your friends know they are not to change their habits on your account. At a proper time and place explain to all your friends why alcohol disagrees with you. If you do this thoroughly, few people will ask you to drink. While you were drinking, you were withdrawing from life little by little. Now you are getting back into the social life of this world. Don't start to withdraw again just because your friends drink liquor.

Your job now is to be at the place where you may be of maximum helpfulness to others, so never hesitate to go anywhere if you can be helpful. You should not hesitate to visit the most sordid spot on earth on such an errand. Keep on the firing line of life with these motives and God will keep you unharmed.

Many of us keep liquor in our homes. We often need it to carry green recruits through a severe hangover Some of us still serve it to our friends provided they are not alcoholic. But some of us think we should not serve liquor to anyone. We never argue this question. We feel that each family, in the light of their own circumstances, ought to decide for themselves.

We are careful never to show intolerance or hatred of drinking as an institution. Experience shows that such an attitude is not helpful to anyone. Every new alcoholic looks for this spirit among us and is immensely relieved when he finds we are not witch burners. A spirit of intolerance might repel alcoholics whose lives could have been saved, had it not been for such stupidity. We would not even do the cause of temperate drinking any good, for not one drinker in a thousand likes to be told anything about alcohol by one who hates it.

Some day we hope that Alcoholics Anonymous will help the public to a better realization of the gravity of the alcoholic problem, but we shall be of little use if our attitude is one of bitterness or hostility. Drinkers will not stand for it.

After all, our problems were of our own making. Bottles were only a symbol. Besides, we have stopped fighting anybody or anything. We have to!

Chapter 8

TO WIVES

WITH FEW EXCEPTIONS, our book thus far has spoken of men. But what we have said applies quite as much to women. Our activities in behalf of women who drink are on the increase. There is every evidence that women regain their health as readily as men if they try our suggestions.

But for every man who drinks others are involved—the wife who trembles in fear of the next debauch; the mother and father who see their son wasting away.

Among us are wives, relatives and friends whose problem has been solved, as well as some who have not yet found a happy solution. We want the wives of Alcoholics Anonymous to address the wives of men who drink too much. What they say will apply to nearly everyone bound by ties of blood or affection to an alcoholic.

As wives of Alcoholics Anonymous, we would like you to feel that we understand as perhaps few can. We want to analyze mistakes we have made. We want to leave you with the feeling that no situation is too difficult and no unhappiness too great to be overcome.

We have traveled a rocky road, there is no mistake about that. We have had long rendezvous with hurt pride, frustration, self-pity, misunderstanding and fear. These are not pleasant companions. We have been driven to maudlin sympathy, to bitter resentment. Some of us veered from extreme to extreme, ever hoping that one day our loved ones would be themselves once more.

Our loyalty and the desire that our husbands hold up their heads and be like other men have begotten all sorts of predicaments. We have been unselfish and self-sacrificing. We have told innumerable lies to protect our pride and our husbands' reputations. We have prayed, we have begged, we have been patient. We have struck out viciously. We have run away. We have been hysterical. We have been terror stricken. We have sought sympathy. We have had retaliatory love affairs with other men.

Our homes have been battle-grounds many an evening. In the morning we have kissed and made up. Our friends have counseled chucking the men and we have done so with finality, only to be back in a little while hoping, always hoping. Our men have sworn great solemn oaths that they were through drinking forever. We have believed them when no one else could or would. Then, in days, weeks, or months, a fresh outburst.

We seldom had friends at our homes, never knowing how or when the men of the house would appear. We could make few social engagements. We came to live almost alone. When we were invited out, our husbands sneaked so many drinks that they spoiled the occasion. If, on the other hand, they took nothing, their self-pity made them killjoys.

There was never financial security. Positions were always in jeopardy or gone. An armored car could not have brought the pay envelopes home. The checking account melted like snow in June.

Sometimes there were other women. How heartbreaking was this discovery; how cruel to be told they understood our men as we did not!

The bill collectors, the sheriffs, the angry taxi drivers, the policemen, the bums, the pals, and even the ladies they sometimes brought home—our husbands thought we were so inhospitable. "Joykiller, nag, wet blanket"—that's what they said. Next day they would be themselves again and we would forgive and try to forget.

We have tried to hold the love of our children for their father. We have told small tots that father was sick, which was much nearer the truth than we realized. They struck the children, kicked out door panels, smashed treasured crockery, and ripped the keys out of pianos. In the midst of such pandemonium they may have rushed out threatening to live with the other woman forever. In desperation, we have even got tight ourselves—the drunk to end all drunks. The unexpected result was that our husbands seemed to like it.

Perhaps at this point we got a divorce and took the children home to father and mother. Then we were severely criticized by our husband's parents for desertion. Usually we did not leave. We stayed on and on. We finally sought employment ourselves as destitution faced us and our families.

We began to ask medical advice as the sprees got closer together. The alarming physical and mental symptoms, the deepening pall of remorse, depression and inferiority that settled down on our loved ones—

these things terrified and distracted us. As animals on a treadmill, we have patiently and wearily climbed, falling back in exhaustion after each futile effort to reach solid ground. Most of us have entered the final stage with its commitment to health resorts, sanitariums, hospitals, and jails. Sometimes there were screaming delirium and insanity. Death was often near.

Under these conditions we naturally made mistakes. Some of them rose out of ignorance of alcoholism. Sometimes we sensed dimly that we were dealing with sick men. Had we fully understood the nature of the alcoholic illness, we might have behaved differently.

How could men who loved their wives and children be so unthinking, so callous, so cruel? There could be no love in such persons, we thought. And just as we were being convinced of their heartlessness, they would surprise us with fresh resolves and new attentions. For a while they would be their old sweet selves, only to dash the new structure of affection to pieces once more. Asked why they commenced to drink again, they would reply with some silly excuse, or none. It was so baffling, so heartbreaking. Could we have been so mistaken in the men we married? When drinking, they were strangers. Sometimes they were so inaccessible that it seemed as though a great wall had been built around them.

And even if they did not love their families, how could they be so blind about themselves? What had become of their judgment, their common sense, their will power? Why could they not see that drink meant ruin to them? Why was it, when these dangers were pointed out that they agreed, and then got drunk again immediately?

These are some of the questions which race through the mind of every woman who has an alcoholic husband. We hope this book has answered some of them. Perhaps your husband has been living in that strange world of alcoholism where everything is distorted and exaggerated. You can see that he really does love you with his better self. Of course, there is such a thing as incompatibility, but in nearly every instance the alcoholic only seems to be unloving and inconsiderate; it is usually because he is warped and sickened that he says and does these appalling things. Today most of our men are better husbands and fathers than ever before.

Try not to condemn your alcoholic husband no matter what he says or does. He is just another very sick, unreasonable person. Treat him, when you can, as though he had pneumonia. When he angers you, remember that he is very ill.

There is an important exception to the foregoing. We realize some men are thoroughly bad-intentioned, that no amount of patience will make any difference. An alcoholic of this temperament may be quick to use this chapter as a club over your head. Don't let him get away with it. If you are positive he is one of this type you may feel you had better leave. Is it right to let him ruin your life and the lives of your children? Especially when he has before him a way to stop his drinking and abuse if he really wants to pay the price.

The problem with which you struggle usually falls within one of four categories:

One: Your husband may be only a heavy drinker.

His drinking may be constant or it may be heavy only on certain occasions. Perhaps he spends too much money for liquor. It may be slowing him up mentally and physically, but he does not see it. Sometimes he is a source of embarrassment to you and his friends. He is positive he can handle his liquor, that it does him no harm, that drinking is necessary in his business. He would probably be insulted if he were called an alcoholic. This world is full of people like him. Some will moderate or stop altogether, and some will not. Of those who keep on, a good number will become true alcoholics after a while.

Two: Your husband is showing lack of control, for he is unable to stay on the water wagon even when he wants to. He often gets entirely out of hand when drinking. He admits this is true, but is positive that he will do better. He has begun to try, with or without your cooperation, various means of moderating or staying dry. Maybe he is beginning to lose his friends. His business may suffer somewhat. He is worried at times, and is becoming aware that he cannot drink like other people. He sometimes drinks in the morning and through the day also, to hold his nervousness in check. He is remorseful after serious drinking bouts and tells you he wants to stop. But when he gets over the spree, he begins to think once more how he can drink moderately next time. We think this person is in danger. These are the earmarks of a real alcoholic. Perhaps he can still tend to business fairly well. He has by no means ruined everything. As we say among ourselves, *"He wants to want to stop."*

Three: This husband has gone much further than husband number two. Though once like number two he became worse. His friends have slipped away, his home is a near-wreck and he cannot hold a position. Maybe the doctor has been called in, and the weary round of sanitariums and hospitals has begun. He admits he cannot drink like other people, but does not see why. He clings to the notion that he will yet find a way to do so. He may have come to the point where he desperately wants to stop but cannot. His case presents additional questions which we shall try to answer for you. You can be quite hopeful of a situation like this.

Four: You may have a husband of whom you completely despair. He has been placed in one institution after another. He is violent, or appears definitely insane when drunk. Sometimes he drinks on the way home from the hospital. Perhaps he has had delirium tremens. Doctors may shake their heads and advise you to have him committed. Maybe you have already been obliged to put him away. This picture may not be as dark as it looks. Many of our husbands were just as far gone. Yet they got well.

Let's now go back to husband number one. Oddly enough, he is often difficult to deal with. He enjoys drinking. It stirs his imagination. His friends feel closer over a highball. Perhaps you enjoy drinking with him yourself when he doesn't go too far. You have passed happy evenings together chatting and drinking before your fire. Perhaps you both like parties which would be dull without liquor. We have enjoyed such evenings ourselves; we had a good time. We know all about liquor as a social lubricant. Some, but not all of us, think it has its advantages when reasonably used.

The first principle of success is that you should never be angry. Even though your husband becomes unbearable and you have to leave him temporarily, you should, if you can, go without rancor. Patience and good temper are most necessary.

Our next thought is that you should never tell him what he must do about his drinking. If he gets the idea that you are a nag or killjoy, your chance of accomplishing anything useful may be zero. He will use that as an excuse to drink more. He will tell you he is misunderstood. This may lead to lonely evenings for you. He may seek someone else to console him—not always another man.

Be determined that your husband's drinking is not going to spoil your relations with your children or your friends. They need your companionship and your help. It is possible to have a full and useful life, though your husband continues to drink. We know women who are unafraid, even happy under these conditions. Do not set your heart on reforming your husband. You may be unable to do so, no matter how hard you try.

We know these suggestions are sometimes difficult to follow, but you will save many a heartbreak if you can succeed in observing them. Your husband may come to appreciate your reasonableness and patience. This may lay the groundwork for a friendly talk about his alcoholic problem. Try to have him bring up the subject himself. Be sure you are not critical during such a discussion. Attempt instead, to put yourself in his place. Let him see that you want to be helpful rather than critical.

When a discussion does arise, you might suggest he

read this book or at least the chapter on alcoholism. Tell him you have been worried, though perhaps needlessly. You think he ought to know the subject better, as everyone should have a clear understanding of the risk he takes if he drinks too much. Show him you have confidence in his power to stop or moderate. Say you do not want to be a wet blanket; that you only want him to take care of his health. Thus you may succeed in interesting him in alcoholism.

He probably has several alcoholics among his own acquaintances. You might suggest that you both take an interest in them. Drinkers like to help other drinkers. Your husband may be willing to talk to one of them.

If this kind of approach does not catch your husband's interest, it may be best to drop the subject, but after a friendly talk your husband will usually revive the topic himself. This may take patient waiting, but it will be worth it. Meanwhile you might try to help the wife of another serious drinker. If you act upon these principles, your husband may stop or moderate.

Suppose, however, that your husband fits the description of number two. The same principles which apply to husband number one should be practiced. But after his next binge, ask him if he would really like to get over drinking for good. Do not ask that he do it for you or anyone else. Just would he *like* to?

The chances are he would. Show him your copy of this book and tell him what you have found out about alcoholism. Show him that as alcoholics, the writers of the book understand. Tell him some of the interesting stories you have read. If you think he will be shy of a spiritual remedy, ask him to look at the chapter on alcoholism. Then perhaps he will be interested enough to continue.

If he is enthusiastic your cooperation will mean a great deal. If he is lukewarm or thinks he is not an alcoholic, we suggest you leave him alone. Avoid urging him to follow our program. The seed has been planted in his mind. He knows that thousands of men, much like himself, have recovered. But don't remind him of this after he had been drinking, for he may be angry. Sooner or later, you are likely to find him reading the book once more. Wait until repeated stumbling convinces him he must act, for the more you hurry him the longer his recovery may be delayed.

If you have a number three husband, you may be in luck. Being certain he wants to stop, you can go to him with this volume as joyfully as though you had struck oil. He may not share your enthusiasm, but he is practically sure to read the book and he may go for the program at once. If he does not, you will probably not have long to wait. Again, you should not crowd him. Let him decide for himself. Cheerfully see him through more sprees. Talk about his condition or this book only when he raises the issue. In some cases it may be better to let someone outside the family present the book. They can urge action without arousing hostility. If your husband is otherwise a normal individual, your chances are good at this stage.

You would suppose that men in the fourth classification would be quite hopeless, but that is not so. Many of Alcoholics Anonymous were like that. Everybody had given them up. Defeat seemed certain. Yet often such men had spectacular and powerful recoveries.

There are exceptions. Some men have been so impaired by alcohol that they cannot stop. Sometimes there are cases where alcoholism is complicated by other disorders. A good doctor or psychiatrist can tell you whether these complications are serious. In any event, try to have your husband read this book. His reaction may be one of enthusiasm. If he is already committed to an institution, but can convince you and your doctor that he means business, give him a chance to try our method, unless the doctor thinks his mental condition too abnormal or dangerous. We make this recommendation with some confidence. For years we have been working with alcoholics committed to institutions. Since this book was first published, A.A. has released thousands of alcoholics from asylums and hospitals of every kind. The majority have never returned. The power of God goes deep!

You may have the reverse situation on your hands. Perhaps you have a husband who is at large, but who should be committed. Some men cannot or will not get over alcoholism. When they become too dangerous, we think the kind thing is to lock them up, but of course a good doctor should always be consulted. The wives and children of such men suffer horribly, but not more than the men themselves.

But sometimes you must start life anew. We know women who have done it. If such women adopt a spiritual way of life their road will be smoother.

If your husband is a drinker, you probably worry over what other people are thinking and you hate to meet your friends. You draw more and more into yourself and you think everyone is talking about conditions at your home. You avoid the subject of drinking, even with your own parents. You do not know what to tell the children. When your husband is bad, you become a trembling recluse, wishing the telephone had never been invented.

We find that most of this embarrassment is unnecessary. While you need not discuss your husband at length, you can quietly let your friends know the nature of his illness. But you must be on guard not to embarrass or harm your husband.

When you have carefully explained to such people that he is a sick person, you will have created a new atmosphere. Barriers which have sprung up between you and your friends will disappear with the growth of sympathetic understanding. You will no longer be self-conscious or feel that you must apologize as though your husband were a weak character. He may be anything but that. Your new courage, good nature and lack of self-consciousness will do wonders for you socially.

The same principle applies in dealing with the children. Unless they actually need protection from their father, it is best not to take sides in any argument he has with them while drinking. Use your energies to promote a better understanding all around. Then that terrible tension which grips the home of every problem drinker will be lessened.

Frequently, you have felt obliged to tell your husband's employer and his friends that he was sick, when as a matter of fact he was tight. Avoid answering these inquiries as much as you can. Whenever possible, let your husband explain. Your desire to protect him should not cause you to lie to people when they have a right to know were he is and what he is doing. Discuss this with him when he is sober and in good spirits. Ask him what you should do if he places you in such a position again. But be careful not to be resentful about the last time he did so.

There is another paralyzing fear. You may be afraid your husband will lose his position; you are thinking of the disgrace and hard times which will befall you and the children. This experience may come to you. Or you may already have had it several times. Should it happen again, regard it in a different light. Maybe it will prove a blessing! It may convince your husband he wants to stop drinking forever. And now you know that he can stop if he will! Time after time, this apparent calamity has been a boon to us, for it opened up a path which led to the discovery of God.

We have elsewhere remarked how much better life is when lived on a spiritual plane. If God can solve the age-old riddle of alcoholism, He can solve your problems too. We wives found that, like everybody else, we were afflicted with pride, self-pity, vanity and all the things which go to make up the self-centered person; and we were not above selfishness or dishonesty. As our husbands began to apply spiritual principles in their lives, we began to see the desirability of doing so too.

At first, some of us did not believe we needed this help. We thought, on the whole, we were pretty good women, capable of being nicer if our husbands stopped drinking. But it was a silly idea that we were too good to need God. Now we try to put spiritual principles to work in every department of our lives. When we do that, we find it solves our problems too; the ensuing lack of fear, worry and hurt feelings is a wonderful thing. We urge you to try our program, for nothing will be so helpful to your husband as the radically changed attitude toward him which God will show you how to have. Go along with your husband if you possibly can.

If you and your husband find a solution for the pressing problem of drink you are, of course, going to be very happy. But all problems will not be solved at once. Seed has started to sprout in a new soil, but growth has only begun. In spite of your new-found happiness, there will be ups and downs. Many of the old problems will still be with you. This is as it should be.

The faith and sincerity of both you and your husband will be put to the test. These work-outs should be regarded as part of your education, for thus you will be learning to live. You will make mistakes, but if you are in earnest they will not drag you down. Instead, you will capitalize them. A better way of life will emerge when they are overcome.

Some of the snags you will encounter are irritation, hurt feelings and resentments. Your husband will sometimes be unreasonable and you will want to criticize. Starting from a speck on the domestic horizon, great thunderclouds of dispute may gather. These family dissensions are very dangerous, especially to your husband. Often you must carry the burden of avoiding them or keeping them under control. Never forget that resentment is a deadly hazard to an alcoholic. We do not mean that you have to agree with your husband whenever there is an honest difference of opinion. Just be careful not to disagree in a resentful or critical spirit.

You and your husband will find that you can dispose of serious problems easier than you can the trivial ones. Next time you and he have a heated discussion, no matter what the subject, it should be the privilege of either to smile and say, "This is getting serious. I'm sorry I got disturbed. Let's talk about it later." If your husband is trying to live on a spiritual basis, he will also be doing everything in his power to avoid disagreement or contention.

Your husband knows he owes you more than sobriety. He wants to make good. Yet you must not expect too much. His ways of thinking and doing are the habits of years. Patience, tolerance, understanding and love are the watchwords. Show him these things in yourself and they will be reflected back to you from him. Live and let live is the rule. If you both show a willingness to remedy your own defects, there will be little need to criticize each other.

We women carry with us a picture of the ideal man, the sort of chap we would like our husbands to be. It is the most natural thing in the world, once his liquor problem is solved, to feel that he will now measure up to that cherished vision. The chances are he will not for, like yourself, he is just beginning his development. Be patient.

Another feeling we are very likely to entertain is one of resentment that love and loyalty could not cure our husbands of alcoholism. We do not like the thought that the contents of a book or the work of another alcoholic has accomplished in a few weeks that for which we struggled for years. At such moments we forget that alcoholism is an illness over which we could not possibly have had any power. Your husband will be the first to say it was your devotion and care which brought him to the point where he could have a spiritual experience. Without you he would have gone to pieces long ago. When resentful thoughts come, try to pause and count your blessings. After all, your family is reunited, alcohol is no longer a problem and you and your husband are working together toward an un-dreamed-of future.

Still another difficulty is that you may become jealous of the attention he bestows on other people, especially alcoholics. You have been starving for his companionship, yet he spends long hours helping other men and their families. You feel he should now be yours. The fact is that he should work with other people to maintain his own sobriety. Sometimes he will be so interested that he becomes really neglectful. Your house is filled with strangers. You may not like some of them. He gets stirred up about their troubles, but not at all about yours. It will do little good if you point that out and urge more attention for yourself. We find it a real mistake to dampen his enthusiasm for alcoholic work. You should join in his efforts as much as you possibly can. We suggest that you direct some of your thought to the wives of his new alcoholic friends. They need the counsel and love of a woman who has gone through what you have.

It is probably true that you and your husband have been living too much alone, for drinking many times isolates the wife of an alcoholic. Therefore, you probably need fresh interests and a great cause to live for as much as your husband. If you cooperate, rather than complain, you will find that his excess enthusiasm will tone down. Both of you will awaken to a new

sense of responsibility for others. You, as well as your
husband, ought to think of what you can put into life
instead of how much you can take out. Inevitably your
lives will be fuller for doing so. You will lose the old
life to find one much better.

Perhaps your husband will make a fair start on the
new basis, but just as things are going beautifully he
dismays you by coming home drunk. If you are satisfied he really wants to get over drinking, you need not
be alarmed. Though it is infinitely better that he have
no relapse at all, as has been true with many of our
men, it is by no means a bad thing in some cases. Your
husband will see at once that he must redouble his spiritual activities if he expects to survive. You need not
remind him of his spiritual deficiency—he will know
of it. Cheer him up and ask him how you can be still
more helpful.

The slightest sign of fear or intolerance may lessen
your husband's chance of recovery. In a weak moment
he may take your dislike of his high-stepping friends
as one of those insanely trivial excuses to drink.

We never, never try to arrange a man's life so as to
shield him from temptation. The slightest disposition
on your part to guide his appointments or his affairs so
he will not be tempted will be noticed. Make him feel
absolutely free to come and go as he likes. This is
important. If he gets drunk, don't blame yourself. God
has either removed your husband's liquor problem or
He has not. If not, it had better be found out right away.
Then you and your husband can get right down to fun-
damentals. If a repetition is to be prevented, place the
problem, along with everything else, in God's hands.

We realize that we have been giving you much direction and advice. We may have seemed to lecture. If that is so we are sorry, for we ourselves don't always care for people who lecture us. But what we have related is based upon experience, some of it painful. We had to learn these things the hard way. That is why we are anxious that you understand, and that you avoid these unnecessary difficulties.

So to you out there—who may soon be with us—we say "Good luck and God bless you!"

Chapter 9

THE FAMILY AFTERWARD

*O*UR WOMEN FOLK have suggested certain attitudes a wife may take with the husband who is recovering. Perhaps they created the impression that he is to be wrapped in cotton wool and placed on a pedestal. Successful readjustment means the opposite. All members of the family should meet upon the common ground of tolerance, understanding and love. This involves a process of deflation. The alcoholic, his wife, his children, his "in-laws," each one is likely to have fixed ideas about the family's attitude towards himself or herself. Each is interested in having his or her wishes respected. We find the more one member of the family demands that the others concede to him, the more resentful they become. This makes for discord and unhappiness.

And why? Is it not because each wants to play the lead? Is not each trying to arrange the family show to his liking? Is he not unconsciously trying to see what he can take from the family life rather than give?

Cessation of drinking is but the first step away from a highly strained, abnormal condition. A doctor said to us, "Years of living with an alcoholic is almost sure to make any wife or child neurotic. The entire family is, to some extent, ill." Let families realize, as they start their journey, that all will not be fair weather. Each in his turn may be footsore and may straggle.

There will be alluring shortcuts and by-paths down which they may wander and lose their way.

Suppose we tell you some of the obstacles a family will meet; suppose we suggest how they may be avoided—even converted to good use for others. The family of an alcoholic longs for the return of happiness and security. They remember when father was romantic, thoughtful and successful. Today's life is measured against that of other years and, when it falls short, the family may be unhappy.

Family confidence in dad is rising high. The good old days will soon be back, they think. Sometimes they demand that dad bring them back instantly! God, they believe, almost owes this recompense on a long over-due account. But the head of the house has spent years in pulling down the structures of business, romance, friendship, health—these things are now ruined or damaged. It will take time to clear away the wreck. Though old buildings will eventually be replaced by finer ones, the new structures will take years to complete.

Father knows he is to blame; it may take him many seasons of hard work to be restored financially, but he shouldn't be reproached. Perhaps he will never have much money again. But the wise family will admire him for what he is trying to be, rather than for what he is trying to get.

Now and then the family will be plagued by spectres from the past, for the drinking career of almost every alcoholic has been marked by escapades, funny, humiliating, shameful or tragic. The first impulse will be to bury these skeletons in a dark closet and padlock the door. The family may be possessed by the idea that future happiness can be based only upon forget-fulness of the past. We think that such a view is self-centered and in direct conflict with the new way of living.

Henry Ford once made a wise remark to the effect that experience is the thing of supreme value in life.[1] That is true only if one is willing to turn the past to good account. We grow by our willingness to face and rectify errors and convert them into assets. The alcoholic's past thus becomes the principal asset of the family and frequently it is almost the only one!

This painful past may be of infinite value to other families still struggling with their problem. We think each family which has been relieved owes something to those who have not, and when the occasion requires, each member of it should be only too willing to bring former mistakes, no matter how grievous, out of their hiding places. Showing others who suffer how we were given help is the very thing which makes life seem so worth while to us now. Cling to the thought that, in God's hands, the dark past is the greatest possession you have—the key to life and happiness for others. With it you can avert death and misery for them.

It is possible to dig up past misdeeds so they become a blight, a veritable plague. For example, we know of situations in which the alcoholic or his wife have had love affairs. In the first flush of spiritual experience they forgave each other and drew closer together. The miracle of reconciliation was at hand. Then, under one provocation or another, the aggrieved one would unearth the old affair and angrily cast its ashes about. A few of us have had these growing pains and they hurt a great deal. Husbands and wives have sometimes been obliged to separate for a time until new perspective, new victory over hurt pride could be re-won. In most cases, the alcoholic survived this ordeal without relapse, but not always. So we think that unless some good and useful purpose is to be served, past occurrences should not be discussed.

We families of Alcoholics Anonymous keep few skeletons in the closet. Everyone knows about the others' alcoholic troubles. This is a condition which, in ordinary life, would produce untold grief; there might be scandalous gossip, laughter at the expense of other people, and a tendency to take advantage of intimate information. Among us, these are rare occurrences. We do talk about each other a great deal, but we almost invariably temper such talk by a spirit of love and tolerance.

Another principle we observe carefully is that we do not relate intimate experiences of another person unless we are sure he would approve. We find it better, when possible, to stick to our own stories. A man may criticize or laugh at himself and it will affect others favorably, but criticism or ridicule coming from another often produces the contrary effect. Members of a family should watch such matters carefully, for one careless, inconsiderate remark has been known to raise the very devil. We alcoholics are sensitive people. It takes some of us a long time to outgrow that serious handicap.

Many alcoholics are enthusiasts. They run to extremes. At the beginning of recovery a man will take, as a rule, one of two directions. He may either plunge into a frantic attempt to get on his feet in business, or he may be so enthralled by his new life that he talks or thinks of little else. In either case certain family problems will arise. With these we have had experience galore.

We think it dangerous if he rushes headlong at his economic problem. The family will be affected also, pleasantly at first, as they feel their money troubles are about to be solved, then not so pleasantly as they find themselves neglected. Dad may be tired at night and preoccupied by day. He may take small interest in the children and may show irritation when reproved for his delinquencies. If not irritable, he may seem dull and boring, not gay and affectionate as the family would like him to be. Mother may complain of inattention. They are all disappointed, and often let him feel it. Beginning with such complaints, a barrier arises. He is straining every nerve to make up for lost time. He is striving to recover fortune and reputation and feels he is doing very well.

Sometimes mother and children don't think so. Having been neglected and misused in the past, they think father owes them more than they are getting. They want him to make a fuss over them. They expect him to give them the nice times they used to have before he drank so much, and to show his contrition for what they suffered. But dad doesn't give freely of himself. Resentment grows. He becomes still less communicative. Sometimes he explodes over a trifle. The family is mystified. They criticize, pointing out how he is falling down on his spiritual program.

This sort of thing can be avoided. Both father and the family are mistaken, though each side may have some justification. It is of little use to argue and only makes the impasse worse. The family must realize that dad, though marvelously improved, is still convalescing. They should be thankful he is sober and able to be of this world once more. Let them praise his progress. Let them remember that his drinking wrought all kinds of damage that may take long to repair. If they sense these things, they will not take so seriously his periods of crankiness, depression, or apathy, which will disappear when there is tolerance, love, and spiritual understanding.

The head of the house ought to remember that he is mainly to blame for what befell his home. He can scarcely square the account in his lifetime. But he must see the danger of over-concentration on financial success. Although financial recovery is on the way for many of us, we found we could not place money first. For us, material well-being always followed spiritual progress; it never preceded.

Since the home has suffered more than anything else, it is well that a man exert himself there. He is not likely to get far in any direction if he fails to show unselfishness and love under his own roof. We know there are difficult wives and families, but the man who is getting over alcoholism must remember he did much to make them so.

As each member of a resentful family begins to see his shortcomings and admits them to the others, he lays a basis for helpful discussion. These family talks will be constructive if they can be carried on without heated argument, self-pity, self-justification or resentful criticism. Little by little, mother and children will see they ask too much, and father will see he gives too little. Giving, rather than getting, will become the guiding principle.

Assume on the other hand that father has, at the outset, a stirring spiritual experience. Overnight, as it were, he is a different man. He becomes a religious enthusiast. He is unable to focus on anything else. As soon as his sobriety begins to be taken as a matter of course, the family may look at their strange new dad with apprehension, then with irritation. There is talk about spiritual matters morning, noon and night. He may demand that the family find God in a hurry, or exhibit amazing indifference to them and say he is above worldly considerations. He may tell mother, who has been religious all her life, that she doesn't know what it's all about, and that she had better get his brand of spirituality while there is yet time.

When father takes this tack, the family may react unfavorably. They may be jealous of a God who has stolen dad's affections. While grateful that he drinks no more, they may not like the idea that God has accomplished the miracle where they failed. They often forget father was beyond human aid. They may not see why their love and devotion did not straighten him out. Dad is not so spiritual after all, they say. If he means to right his past wrongs, why all this concern for everyone in the world but his family? What about his talk that God will take care of them? They suspect father is a bit balmy!

He is not so unbalanced as they might think. Many of us have experienced dad's elation. We have indulged in spiritual intoxication. Like a gaunt prospector, belt drawn in over the last ounce of food, our pick struck gold. Joy at our release from a lifetime of frustration knew no bounds. Father feels he has struck something better than gold. For a time he may try to hug the new treasure to himself. He may not see at once that he has barely scratched a limitless lode which will pay dividends only if he mines it for the rest of his life and insists on giving away the entire product.

If the family cooperates, dad will soon see that he is suffering from a distortion of values. He will perceive that his spiritual growth is lopsided, that for an average man like himself, a spiritual life which does not include his family obligations may not be so perfect after all. If the family will appreciate that dad's current behavior is but a phase of his development, all will be well. In the midst of an understanding and sympathetic family, these vagaries of dad's spiritual infancy will quickly disappear.

The opposite may happen should the family condemn and criticize. Dad may feel that for years his drinking has placed him on the wrong side of every argument, but that now he has become a superior person with God on his side. If the family persists in criticism, this fallacy may take a still greater hold on father. Instead of treating the family as he should, he may retreat further into himself and feel he has spiritual justification for so doing.

Though the family does not fully agree with dad's spiritual activities, they should let him have his head. Even if he displays a certain amount of neglect and irresponsibility towards the family, it is well to let him go as far as he likes in helping other alcoholics. During those first days of convalescence, this will do more to insure his sobriety than anything else. Though some of his manifestations are alarming and disagreeable, we think dad will be on a firmer foundation than the man who is placing business or professional success ahead of spiritual development. He will be less likely to drink again, and anything is preferable to that.

Those of us who have spent much time in the world of spiritual make-believe have eventually seen the childishness of it. This dream world has been replaced by a great sense of purpose, accompanied by a growing consciousness of the power of God in our lives. We have come to believe He would like us to keep our heads in the clouds with Him, but that our feet ought to be firmly planted on earth. That is where our fellow travelers are, and that is where our work must be done. These are the realities for us. We have found nothing incompatible between a powerful spiritual experience and a life of sane and happy usefulness.

One more suggestion: Whether the family has spiritual convictions or not, they may do well to examine the principles by which the alcoholic member is trying to live. They can hardly fail to approve these simple principles, though the head of the house still fails somewhat in practicing them. Nothing will help the man who is off on a spiritual tangent so much as the wife who adopts a sane spiritual program, making a better practical use of it.

There will be other profound changes in the household. Liquor incapacitated father for so many years that mother became head of the house. She met these responsibilities gallantly. By force of circumstances, she was often obliged to treat father as a sick or wayward child. Even when he wanted to assert himself he could not, for his drinking placed him constantly in the wrong. Mother made all the plans and gave the directions. When sober, father usually obeyed. Thus mother, through no fault of her own, became accustomed to wearing the family trousers. Father, coming suddenly to life again, often begins to assert himself. This means trouble, unless the family watches for these tendencies in each other and comes to a friendly agreement about them.

Drinking isolates most homes from the outside world. Father may have laid aside for years all normal activities—clubs, civic duties, sports. When he renews interest in such things, a feeling of jealousy may arise. The family may feel they hold a mortgage on dad, so big that no equity should be left for outsiders. Instead of developing new channels of activity for themselves, mother and children demand that he stay home and make up the deficiency.

At the very beginning, the couple ought to frankly face the fact that each will have to yield here and there if the family is going to play an effective part in the new life. Father will necessarily spend much time with other alcoholics, but this activity should be balanced. New acquaintances who know nothing of alcoholism might be made and thoughtful consideration given their needs. The problems of the community might engage attention. Though the family has no religious connections, they may wish to make contact with or take membership in a religious body.

Alcoholics who have derided religious people will be helped by such contacts. Being possessed of a spiritual experience, the alcoholic will find he has much in common with these people, though he may differ with them on many matters. If he does not argue about religion, he will make new friends and is sure to find new avenues of usefulness and pleasure. He and his family can be a bright spot in such congregations. He may bring new hope and new courage to many a priest, minister, or rabbi, who gives his all to minister to our troubled world. We intend the foregoing as a helpful suggestion only. So far as we are concerned, there is nothing obligatory about it. As non-denominational people, we cannot make up others' minds for them. Each individual should consult his own conscience.

We have been speaking to you of serious, sometimes tragic things. We have been dealing with alcohol in its worst aspect. But we aren't a glum lot. If newcomers could see no joy or fun in our existence, they wouldn't want it. We absolutely insist on enjoying life. We try not to indulge in cynicism over the state of the nations, nor do we carry the world's troubles on our shoulders. When we see a man sinking into the mire that is alcoholism, we give him first aid and place what we have at his disposal. For his sake, we do recount and almost relive the horrors of our past. But those of us who have tried to shoulder the entire burden and trouble of others find we are soon overcome by them.

So we think cheerfulness and laughter make for usefulness. Outsiders are sometimes shocked when we burst into merriment over a seemingly tragic experience out of the past. But why shouldn't we laugh? We have recovered, and have been given the power to help others.

Everybody knows that those in bad health, and those who seldom play, do not laugh much. So let each family play together or separately, as much as their circumstances warrant. We are sure God wants us to be happy, joyous, and free. We cannot subscribe to the belief that this life is a vale of tears, though it once was just that for many of us. But it is clear that we made our own misery. God didn't do it. Avoid then, the deliberate manufacture of misery, but if trouble comes, cheerfully capitalize it as an opportunity to demonstrate His omnipotence.

Now about health: A body badly burned by alcohol does not often recover overnight nor do twisted thinking and depression vanish in a twinkling. We are convinced that a spiritual mode of living is a most powerful health restorative. We, who have recovered from serious drinking, are miracles of mental health. But we have seen remarkable transformations in our bodies. Hardly one of our crowd now shows any mark of dissipation.

But this does not mean that we disregard human health measures. God has abundantly supplied this world with fine doctors, psychologists, and practitioners of various kinds. Do not hesitate to take your health problems to such persons. Most of them give freely of themselves, that their fellows may enjoy sound minds and bodies. Try to remember that though God has wrought miracles among us, we should never belittle a good doctor or psychiatrist. Their services are often indispensable in treating a newcomer and in following his case afterward.

One of the many doctors who had the opportunity of reading this book in manuscript form told us that the use of sweets was often helpful, of course depending upon a doctor's advice. He thought all alcoholics should constantly have chocolate available for its quick energy value at times of fatigue. He added that occasionally in the night a vague craving arose which would be satisfied by candy. Many of us have noticed a tendency to eat sweets and have found this practice beneficial.

A word about sex relations. Alcohol is so sexually stimulating to some men that they have over-indulged. Couples are occasionally dismayed to find that when drinking is stopped the man tends to be impotent. Unless the reason is understood, there may be an emotional upset. Some of us had this experience, only to enjoy, in a few months, a finer intimacy than ever. There should be no hesitancy in consulting a doctor or psychologist if the condition persists. We do not know of many cases where this difficulty lasted long.

The alcoholic may find it hard to re-establish friendly relations with his children. Their young minds were impressionable while he was drinking. Without saying so, they may cordially hate him for what he has done to them and to their mother. The children are sometimes dominated by a pathetic hardness and cynicism. They cannot seem to forgive and forget. This may hang on for months, long after their mother has accepted dad's new way of living and thinking.

In time they will see that he is a new man and in their own way they will let him know it. When this happens, they can be invited to join in morning meditation and then they can take part in the daily discussion without rancor or bias. From that point on, progress will be rapid. Marvelous results often follow such a reunion.

Whether the family goes on a spiritual basis or not, the alcoholic member has to if he would recover. The others must be convinced of his new status beyond the shadow of a doubt. Seeing is believing to most families who have lived with a drinker.

Here is a case in point: One of our friends is a heavy smoker and coffee drinker. There was no doubt he overindulged. Seeing this, and meaning to be helpful, his wife commenced to admonish him about it. He admitted he was overdoing these things, but frankly said that he was not ready to stop. His wife is one of those persons who really feels there is something rather sinful about these commodities, so she nagged, and her intolerance finally threw him into a fit of anger. He got drunk.

Of course our friend was wrong—dead wrong. He had to painfully admit that and mend his spiritual fences. Though he is now a most effective member of Alcoholics Anonymous, he still smokes and drinks coffee, but neither his wife nor anyone else stands in judgment. She sees she was wrong to make a burning issue out of such a matter when his more serious ailments were being rapidly cured.

We have three little mottoes which are apropos. Here they are:

> *First Things First*
> *Live and Let Live*
> *Easy Does It.*

Note	Page	
1	124	Henry Ford: A pioneer of automated production, became widely known and very wealthy from manufacturing automobiles.

Chapter 10

TO EMPLOYERS

*A*MONG MANY employers nowadays, we think of one member who has spent much of his life in the world of big business. He has hired and fired hundreds of men. He knows the alcoholic as the employer sees him. His present views ought to prove exceptionally useful to business men everywhere.

But let him tell you:

I was at one time assistant manager of a corporation department employing sixty-six hundred men. One day my secretary came in saying that Mr. B— insisted on speaking with me. I told her to say that I was not interested. I had warned him several times that he had but one more chance. Not long afterward he had called me from Hartford on two successive days, so drunk he could hardly speak. I told him he was through—finally and forever.

My secretary returned to say that it was not Mr. B— on the phone; it was Mr. B—'s brother, and he wished to give me a message. I still expected a plea for clemency, but these words came through the receiver: "I just wanted to tell you Paul jumped from a hotel window in Hartford last Saturday. He left us a note saying you were the best boss he ever had, and that you were not to blame in any way."

Another time, as I opened a letter which lay on my

desk, a newspaper clipping fell out. It was the obituary of one of the best salesmen I ever had. After two weeks of drinking, he had placed his toe on the trigger of a loaded shotgun—the barrel was in his mouth. I had discharged him for drinking six weeks before.

Still another experience: A woman's voice came faintly over long distance from Virginia. She wanted to know if her husband's company insurance was still in force. Four days before he had hanged himself in his woodshed. I had been obliged to discharge him for drinking, though he was brilliant, alert, and one of the best organizers I have ever known.

Here were three exceptional men lost to this world because I did not understand alcoholism as I do now. What irony—I became an alcoholic myself! And but for the intervention of an understanding person, I might have followed in their footsteps. My downfall cost the business community unknown thousands of dollars, for it takes real money to train a man for an executive position. This kind of waste goes on unabated. We think the business fabric is shot through with a situation which might be helped by better understanding all around.

Nearly every modern employer feels a moral responsibility for the well-being of his help, and he tries to meet these responsibilities. That he has not always done so for the alcoholic is easily understood. To him the alcoholic has often seemed a fool of the first magnitude. Because of the employee's special ability, or of his own strong personal attachment to him, the employer has sometimes kept such a man at work long beyond a reasonable period. Some employers have tried every known remedy. In only a few instances has there been a lack of patience and tolerance. And we, who have imposed on the best of employers, can scarcely blame them if they have been short with us.

Here, for instance, is a typical example: An officer of one of the largest banking institutions in America knows I no longer drink. One day he told me about an executive of the same bank who, from his description, was undoubtedly alcoholic. This seemed to me like an opportunity to be helpful, so I spent two hours talking about alcoholism, the malady, and described the symptoms and results as well as I could. His comment was, "Very interesting. But I'm sure this man is done drinking. He has just returned from a three-months leave of absence, has taken a cure, looks fine, and to clinch the matter, the board of directors told him this was his last chance."

The only answer I could make was that if the man followed the usual pattern, he would go on a bigger bust than ever. I felt this was inevitable and wondered if the bank was doing the man an injustice. Why not bring him into contact with some of our alcoholic crowd? He might have a chance. I pointed out that I had had nothing to drink whatever for three years, and this in the face of difficulties that would have made nine out of ten men drink their heads off. Why not at least afford him an opportunity to hear my story? "Oh no," said my friend, "this chap is either through with liquor, or he is minus a job. If he has your will power and guts, he will make the grade."

I wanted to throw up my hands in discouragement, for I saw that I had failed to help my banker friend understand. He simply could not believe that his brother-executive suffered from a serious illness. There was nothing to do but wait.

Presently the man did slip and was fired. Following his discharge, we contacted him. Without much ado, he accepted the principles and procedure that had helped us. He is undoubtedly on the road to recovery. To me, this incident illustrates lack of understanding as to what really ails the alcoholic, and lack of knowledge as to what part employers might profitably take in salvaging their sick employees.

If you desire to help it might be well to disregard your own drinking, or lack of it. Whether you are a hard drinker, a moderate drinker or a teetotaler, you may have some pretty strong opinions, perhaps prejudices.[1] Those who drink moderately may be more annoyed with an alcoholic than a total abstainer would be. Drinking occasionally, and understanding your own reactions, it is possible for you to become quite sure of many things which, so far as the alcoholic is concerned, are not always so. As a moderate drinker, you can take your liquor or leave it alone. Whenever you want to, you control your drinking. Of an evening, you can go on a mild bender, get up in the morning, shake your head and go to business. To you, liquor is no real problem. You cannot see why it should be to anyone else, save the spineless and stupid.

When dealing with an alcoholic, there may be a natural annoyance that a man could be so weak, stupid and irresponsible. Even when you understand the malady better, you may feel this feeling rising.

A look at the alcoholic in your organization is many times illuminating. Is he not usually brilliant, fast-thinking, imaginative and likeable? When sober, does he not work hard and have a knack of getting things done? If he had these qualities and did not drink would he be worth retaining? Should he have the same consideration as other ailing employees? Is he worth salvaging? If your decision is yes, whether the reason be humanitarian or business or both, then the following suggestions may be helpful.

Can you discard the feeling that you are dealing only with habit, with stubbornness, or a weak will? If this presents difficulty, re-reading chapters two and three, where the alcoholic sickness is discussed at length might be worth while. You, as a business man, want to know the necessities before considering the result. If you concede that your employee is ill, can he be forgiven for what he has done in the past? Can his past absurdities be forgotten? Can it be appreciated that he has been a victim of crooked thinking, directly caused by the action of alcohol on his brain?

I well remember the shock I received when a prominent doctor in Chicago told me of cases where pressure of the spinal fluid actually ruptured the brain. No wonder an alcoholic is strangely irrational. Who wouldn't be, with such a fevered brain? Normal drinkers are not so affected, nor can they understand the aberrations of the alcoholic.

Your man has probably been trying to conceal a number of scrapes, perhaps pretty messy ones. They may be disgusting. You may be at a loss to understand how such a seemingly above-board chap could be so involved. But these scrapes can generally be charged, no matter how bad, to the abnormal action of alcohol on his mind. When drinking, or getting over a bout, an alcoholic, sometimes the model of honesty when

normal, will do incredible things. Afterward, his revulsion will be terrible. Nearly always, these antics
indicate nothing more than temporary conditions.

This is not to say that all alcoholics are honest and
upright when not drinking. Of course that isn't so, and
such people often may impose on you. Seeing your
attempt to understand and help, some men will try to
take advantage of your kindness. If you are sure your
man does not want to stop, he may as well be discharged, the sooner the better. You are not doing him a
favor by keeping him on. Firing such an individual
may prove a blessing to him. It may be just the jolt he
needs. I know, in my own particular case, that nothing
my company could have done would have stopped me
for, so long as I was able to hold my position, I could
not possibly realize how serious my situation was. Had
they fired me first, and had they then taken steps to see
that I was presented with the solution contained in this
book, I might have returned to them six months later, a
well man.

But there are many men who want to stop, and with
them you can go far. Your understanding treatment of
their cases will pay dividends.

Perhaps you have such a man in mind. He wants to
quit drinking and you want to help him, even if it be
only a matter of good business. You now know more
about alcoholism. You can see that he is mentally and
physically sick. You are willing to overlook his past
performances. Suppose an approach is made something like this:

State that you know about his drinking, and that it
must stop. You might say you appreciate his abilities,
would like to keep him, but cannot if he continues to

drink. A firm attitude at this point has helped many of us.

Next he can be assured that you do not intend to lecture, moralize, or condemn; that if this was done formerly, it was because of misunderstanding. If possible express a lack of hard feeling toward him. At this point, it might be well to explain alcoholism, the illness. Say that you believe he is a gravely ill person, with this qualification—being perhaps fatally ill, does he want to get well? You ask, because many alcoholics, being warped and drugged, do not want to quit. But does he? Will he take every necessary step, submit to anything to get well, to stop drinking forever?

If he says yes, does he really mean it, or down inside does he think he is fooling you, and that after rest and treatment he will be able to get away with a few drinks now and then? We believe a man should be thoroughly probed on these points. Be satisfied he is not deceiving himself or you.

Whether you mention this book is a matter for your discretion. If he temporizes and still thinks he can ever drink again, even beer, he might as well be discharged after the next bender which, if an alcoholic, he is almost certain to have. He should understand that emphatically. Either you are dealing with a man who can and will get well or you are not. If not, why waste time with him? This may seem severe, but it is usually the best course.

After satisfying yourself that your man wants to recover and that he will go to any extreme to do so, you may suggest a definite course of action. For most alcoholics who are drinking, or who are just getting over a spree, a certain amount of physical treatment is desirable, even imperative. The matter of physical treatment should, of course, be referred to your own doctor. Whatever the method, its object is to thoroughly clear mind and body of the effects of alcohol. In competent hands, this seldom takes long nor is it very expensive. Your man will fare better if placed in such physical condition that he can think straight and no longer craves liquor. If you propose such a procedure to him, it may be necessary to advance the cost of treatment, but we believe it should be made plain that any expense will later be deducted from his pay. It is better for him to feel fully responsible.

If your man accepts your offer, it should be pointed out that physical treatment is but a small part of the picture. Though you are providing him with the best possible medical attention, he should understand that he must undergo a change of heart. To get over drinking will require a transformation of thought and attitude. We all had to place recovery above everything, for without recovery we would have lost both home and business.

Can you have every confidence in his ability to recover? While on the subject of confidence, can you adopt the attitude that so far as you are concerned this will be a strictly personal matter, that his alcoholic derelictions, the treatment about to be undertaken, will never be discussed without his consent? It might be well to have a long chat with him on his return.

To return to the subject matter of this book: It contains full suggestions by which the employee may solve his problem. To you, some of the ideas which it contains are novel. Perhaps you are not quite in sympathy with the approach we suggest. By no means do we offer it as the last word on this subject, but so far as we are concerned, it has worked with us. After all, are you not looking for results rather than methods? Whether your employee likes it or not, he will learn the grim truth about alcoholism. That won't hurt him a bit, even though he does not go for this remedy.

We suggest you draw the book to the attention of the doctor who is to attend your patient during treatment. If the book is read the moment the patient is able, while acutely depressed, realization of his condition may come to him.

We hope the doctor will tell the patient the truth about his condition, whatever that happens to be. When the man is presented with this volume it is best that no one tell him he must abide by its suggestions. The man must decide for himself.

You are betting, of course, that your changed attitude plus the contents of this book will turn the trick. In some cases it will, and in others it may not. But we think that if you persevere, the percentage of successes will gratify you. As our work spreads and our numbers increase, we hope your employees may be put in personal contact with some of us. Meanwhile, we are sure a great deal can be accomplished by the use of the book alone.

On your employee's return, talk with him. Ask him if he thinks he has the answer. If he feels free to discuss his problems with you, if he knows you understand and will not be upset by anything he wishes to say, he will probably be off to a fast start.

In this connection, can you remain undisturbed if the man proceeds to tell you shocking things? He may, for example, reveal that he has padded his expense account or that he has planned to take your best customers away from you. In fact, he may say almost anything if he has accepted our solution which, as you know, demands rigorous honesty. Can you charge this off as you would a bad account and start fresh with him? If he owes you money you may wish to make terms.

If he speaks of his home situation, you can undoubtedly make helpful suggestions. Can he talk frankly with you so long as he does not bear business tales or criticize his associates? With this kind of employee such an attitude will command undying loyalty.

The greatest enemies of us alcoholics are resentment, jealousy, envy, frustration, and fear. Wherever men are gathered together in business there will be rivalries and, arising out of these, a certain amount of office politics. Sometimes we alcoholics have an idea that people are trying to pull us down. Often this is not so at all. But sometimes our drinking will be used politically.

One instance comes to mind in which a malicious individual was always making friendly little jokes about an alcoholic's drinking exploits. In this way he was slyly carrying tales. In another case, an alcoholic was sent to a hospital for treatment. Only a few knew of it at first but, within a short time, it was billboarded throughout the entire company. Naturally this sort of thing decreased the man's chance of recovery. The employer can many times protect the victim from this kind of talk. The employer cannot play favorites, but he can always defend a man from needless provocation and unfair criticism.

As a class, alcoholics are energetic people. They work hard and they play hard. Your man should be on his mettle to make good. Being somewhat weakened, and faced with physical and mental readjustment to a life which knows no alcohol, he may overdo. You may have to curb his desire to work sixteen hours a day. You may need to encourage him to play once in a while. He may wish to do a lot for other alcoholics and something of the sort may come up during business hours. A reasonable amount of latitude will be helpful. This work is necessary to maintain his sobriety.

After your man has gone along without drinking for a few months, you may be able to make use of his services with other employees who are giving you the alcoholic run-around—provided, of course, they are willing to have a third party in the picture. An alcoholic who has recovered, but holds a relatively unimportant job, can talk to a man with a better position. Being on a radically different basis of life, he will never take advantage of the situation.

Your man may be trusted. Long experience with alcoholic excuses naturally arouses suspicion. When his wife next calls saying he is sick, you might jump to the conclusion he is drunk. If he is, and is still trying to recover, he will tell you about it even if it means the loss of his job. For he knows he must be honest if he would live at all. He will appreciate knowing you are not bothering your head about him, that you are not suspicious nor are you trying to run his life so he will be shielded from temptation to drink. If he is conscientiously following the program of recovery he can go anywhere your business may call him.

In case he does stumble, even once, you will have to decide whether to let him go. If you are sure he doesn't mean business, there is no doubt you should discharge him. If, on the contrary, you are sure he is doing his utmost, you may wish to give him another chance. But you should feel under no obligation to keep him on, for your obligation has been well discharged already.

There is another thing you might wish to do. If your organization is a large one, your junior executives might be provided with this book. You might let them know you have no quarrel with the alcoholics of your organization. These juniors are often in a difficult position. Men under them are frequently their friends. So, for one reason or another, they cover these men, hoping matters will take a turn for the better. They often jeopardize their own positions by trying to help serious drinkers who should have been fired long ago, or else given an opportunity to get well.

After reading this book, a junior executive can go to such a man and say approximately this, "Look here, Ed. Do you want to stop drinking or not? You put me on the spot every time you get drunk. It isn't fair to me or the firm. I have been learning something about alcoholism. If you are an alcoholic, you are a mighty sick man. You act like one. The firm wants to help you get over it, and if you are interested, there is a way out. If you take it, your past will be forgotten

and the fact that you went away for treatment will not
be mentioned. But if you cannot or will not stop drinking, I think you ought to resign."

Your junior executive may not agree with the contents of our book. He need not, and often should not
show it to his alcoholic prospect. But at least he will
understand the problem and will no longer be misled
by ordinary promises. He will be able to take a position with such a man which is eminently fair and square.
He will have no further reason for covering up an alcoholic employee.

It boils right down to this: No man should be fired
just because he is alcoholic. If he wants to stop, he
should be afforded a real chance. If he cannot or does
not want to stop, he should be discharged. The exceptions are few.

We think this method of approach will accomplish
several things. It will permit the rehabilitation of good
men. At the same time you will feel no reluctance to
rid yourself of those who cannot or will not stop. Alcoholism may be causing your organization considerable damage in its waste of time, men and reputation.
We hope our suggestions will help you plug up this
sometimes serious leak. We think we are sensible when
we urge that you stop this waste and give your worthwhile man a chance.

The other day an approach was made to the vice president of a large industrial concern. He remarked: "I'm
mighty glad you fellows got over your drinking. But
the policy of this company is not to interfere with the
habits of our employees. If a man drinks so much that
his job suffers, we fire him. I don't see how you can be
of any help to us for, as you see, we don't have

any alcoholic problem." This same company spends millions for research every year. Their cost of production is figured to a fine decimal point. They have recreational facilities. There is company insurance. There is a real interest, both humanitarian and business, in the well-being of employees. But alcoholism—well, they just don't believe they have it.

Perhaps this is a typical attitude. We, who have collectively seen a great deal of business life, at least from the alcoholic angle, had to smile at this gentleman's sincere opinion. He might be shocked if he knew how much alcoholism is costing his organization a year. That company may harbor many actual or potential alcoholics. We believe that managers of large enterprises often have little idea how prevalent this problem is. Even if you feel your organization has no alcoholic problem, it might pay to take another look down the line. You may make some interesting discoveries.

Of course, this chapter refers to alcoholics, sick people, deranged men. What our friend, the vice president, had in mind was the habitual or whoopee drinker. As to them, his policy is undoubtedly sound, but he did not distinguish between such people and the alcoholic.

It is not to be expected that an alcoholic employee will receive a disproportionate amount of time and attention. He should not be made a favorite. The right kind of man, the kind who recovers, will not want this sort of thing. He will not impose. Far from it. He will work like the devil and thank you to his dying day.

Today I own a little company. There are two

alcoholic employees, who produce as much as five normal salesmen. But why not? They have a new attitude, and they have been saved from a living death. I have enjoyed every moment spent in getting them straightened out.

Note	Page	
1	139	teetotaler: a person who does not drink alcohol.

Chapter 11

A VISION FOR YOU

*F*OR MOST normal folks, drinking means conviviality, companionship and colorful imagination. It means release from care, boredom and worry. It is joyous intimacy with friends and a feeling that life is good. But not so with us in those last days of heavy drinking. The old pleasures were gone. They were but memories. Never could we recapture the great moments of the past. There was an insistent yearning to enjoy life as we once did and a heartbreaking obsession that some new miracle of control would enable us to do it. There was always one more attempt—and one more failure.

The less people tolerated us, the more we withdrew from society, from life itself. As we became subjects of King Alcohol, shivering denizens of his mad realm, the chilling vapor that is loneliness settled down. It thickened, ever becoming blacker. Some of us sought out sordid places, hoping to find understanding companionship and approval. Momentarily we did—then would come oblivion and the awful awakening to face the hideous Four Horsemen—Terror, Bewilderment, Frustration, Despair. Unhappy drinkers who read this page will understand!

Now and then a serious drinker, being dry at the moment says, "I don't miss it at all. Feel better. Work better. Having a better time." As ex-problem drinkers, we smile at such a sally. We know our friend is like a boy whistling in the dark to keep up his spirits. He fools himself. Inwardly he would give anything to take half a dozen drinks and get away with them. He will presently try the old game again, for he isn't happy about his sobriety. He cannot picture life without alcohol. Some day he will be unable to imagine life either with alcohol or without it. Then he will know loneliness such as few do. He will be at the jumping-off place. He will wish for the end.

We have shown how we got out from under. You say, "Yes, I'm willing. But am I to be consigned to a life where I shall be stupid, boring and glum, like some righteous people I see? I know I must get along without liquor, but how can I? Have you a sufficient substitute?"

Yes, there is a substitute and it is vastly more than that. It is a fellowship in Alcoholics Anonymous. There you will find release from care, boredom and worry. Your imagination will be fired. Life will mean something at last. The most satisfactory years of your existence lie ahead. Thus we find the fellowship, and so will you.

"How is that to come about?" you ask. "Where am I to find these people?"

You are going to meet these new friends in your own community. Near you, alcoholics are dying helplessly like people in a sinking ship. If you live in a large place, there are hundreds. High and low, rich and poor, these are future fellows of Alcoholics Anonymous. Among them you will make lifelong friends. You will be bound to them with new and wonderful ties, for you will escape disaster together and you will commence shoulder to shoulder your common journey. Then you will know what it means to give of yourself that others may survive and rediscover life. You will learn the full meaning of "Love thy neighbor as thyself."

It may seem incredible that these men are to become happy, respected, and useful once more. How can they rise out of such misery, bad repute and hopelessness? The practical answer is that since these things have happened among us, they can happen with you. Should you wish them above all else, and be willing to make use of our experience, we are sure they will come. The age of miracles is still with us. Our own recovery proves that!

Our hope is that when this chip of a book is launched on the world tide of alcoholism, defeated drinkers will seize upon it, to follow its suggestions. Many, we are sure, will rise to their feet and march on. They will approach still other sick ones and fellowships of Alcoholics Anonymous may spring up in each city and hamlet, havens for those who must find a way out.

In the chapter "Working With Others" you gathered an idea of how we approach and aid others to health. Suppose now that through you several families have adopted this way of life. You will want to know more of how to proceed from that point. Perhaps the best way of treating you to a glimpse of your future will be to describe the growth of the fellowship among us. Here is a brief account:

Years ago, in 1935, one of our number made a journey to a certain western city. From a business standpoint, his trip came off badly. Had he been successful in his enterprise, he would have been set on his feet financially which, at the time, seemed vitally important. But his venture wound up in a law suit and bogged down completely. The proceeding was shot through with much hard feeling and controversy.

Bitterly discouraged, he found himself in a strange place, discredited and almost broke. Still physically weak, and sober but a few months, he saw that his predicament was dangerous. He wanted so much to talk with someone, but whom?

One dismal afternoon he paced a hotel lobby wondering how his bill was to be paid. At one end of the room stood a glass covered directory of local churches. Down the lobby a door opened into an attractive bar. He could see the gay crowd inside. In there he would find companionship and release. Unless he took some drinks, he might not have the courage to scrape an acquaintance and would have a lonely week-end.

Of course he couldn't drink, but why not sit hopefully at a table, a bottle of ginger ale before him? After all, had he not been sober six months now? Perhaps he could handle, say, three drinks—no more! Fear gripped him. He was on thin ice. Again it was the old, insidious insanity—that first drink. With a shiver, he turned away and walked down the lobby to the church directory. Music and gay chatter still floated to him from the bar.

But what about his responsibilities—his family and the men who would die because they would not know how to get well, ah—yes, those other alcoholics? There must be many such in this town. He would phone a clergyman. His sanity returned and he thanked

God. Selecting a church at random from the directory, he stepped into a booth and lifted the receiver.

His call to the clergyman led him presently to a certain resident of the town, who, though formerly able and respected, was then nearing the nadir of alcoholic despair. It was the usual situation: home in jeopardy, wife ill, children distracted, bills in arrears and standing damaged. He had a desperate desire to stop, but saw no way out, for he had earnestly tried many avenues of escape. Painfully aware of being somehow abnormal, the man did not fully realize what it meant to be alcoholic.*

When our friend related his experience, the man agreed that no amount of will power he might muster could stop his drinking for long. A spiritual experience, he conceded, was absolutely necessary, but the price seemed high upon the basis suggested. He told how he lived in constant worry about those who might find out about his alcoholism. He had, of course, the familiar alcoholic obsession that few knew of his drinking. Why, he argued, should he lose the remainder of his business, only to bring still more suffering to his family by foolishly admitting his plight to people from whom he made his livelihood? He would do anything, he said, but that.

Being intrigued, however, he invited our friend to his home. Some time later, and just as he thought he was getting control of his liquor situation, he went on a roaring bender. For him, this was the spree that ended all sprees. He saw that he would have to face

---

* This refers to Bill's first visit with Dr. Bob. These men later became co-founders of A.A. This resulted in A.A.'s first group in Akron, Ohio in 1935.

his problems squarely that God might give him mastery.

One morning he took the bull by the horns and set out to tell those he feared what his trouble had been. He found himself surprisingly well received, and learned that many knew of his drinking. Stepping into his car, he made the rounds of people he had hurt. He trembled as he went about, for this might mean ruin, particularly to a person in his line of business.

At midnight he came home exhausted, but very happy. He has not had a drink since. As we shall see, he now means a great deal to his community, and the major liabilities of thirty years of hard drinking have been repaired in four.

But life was not easy for the two friends. Plenty of difficulties presented themselves. Both saw that they must keep spiritually active. One day they called up the head nurse of a local hospital. They explained their need and inquired if she had a first class alcoholic prospect.

She replied, "Yes, we've got a corker. He's just beaten up a couple of nurses. Goes off his head completely when he's drinking. But he's a grand chap when he's sober, though he's been in here eight times in the last six months. Understand he was once a well-known lawyer in town, but just now we've got him strapped down tight." *

Here was a prospect all right but, by the description, none too promising. The use of spiritual principles in

* This refers to Bill's and Dr. Bob's first visit to A.A. Number Three.

such cases was not so well understood as it is now. But one of the friends said, "Put him in a private room. We'll be down."

Two days later, a future fellow of Alcoholics Anonymous stared glassily at the strangers beside his bed. "Who are you fellows, and why this private room? I was always in a ward before."

Said one of the visitors, "We're giving you a treatment for alcoholism."

Hopelessness was written large on the man's face as he replied, "Oh, but that's no use. Nothing would fix me. I'm a goner. The last three times, I got drunk on the way home from here. I'm afraid to go out the door. I can't understand it."

For an hour, the two friends told him about their drinking experiences. Over and over, he would say: "That's me. That's me. I drink like that."

The man in the bed was told of the acute poisoning from which he suffered, how it deteriorates the body of an alcoholic and warps his mind. There was much talk about the mental state preceding the first drink.

"Yes, that's me," said the sick man, "the very image. You fellows know your stuff all right, but I don't see what good it'll do. You fellows are somebody. I was once, but I'm a nobody now. From what you tell me, I know more than ever I can't stop." At this both the visitors burst into a laugh. Said the future Fellow Anonymous: "Damn little to laugh about that I can see."

The two friends spoke of their spiritual experience and told him about the course of action they carried out.

He interrupted: "I used to be strong for the church,

but that won't fix it. I've prayed to God on hangover mornings and sworn that I'd never touch another drop but by nine o'clock I'd be boiled as an owl."

Next day found the prospect more receptive. He had been thinking it over. "Maybe you're right," he said. "God ought to be able to do anything." Then he added, "He sure didn't do much for me when I was trying to fight this booze racket alone."

On the third day the lawyer gave his life to the care and direction of his Creator, and said he was perfectly willing to do anything necessary. His wife came, scarcely daring to be hopeful, though she thought she saw something different about her husband already. He had begun to have a spiritual experience.

That afternoon he put on his clothes and walked from the hospital a free man. He entered a political campaign, making speeches, frequenting men's gathering places of all sorts, often staying up all night. He lost the race by only a narrow margin. But he had found God—and in finding God had found himself.

That was in June, 1935. He never drank again. He too, has become a respected and useful member of his community. He has helped other men recover, and is a power in the church from which he was long absent.

So, you see, there were three alcoholics in that town, who now felt they had to give to others what they had found, or be sunk. After several failures to find others, a fourth turned up. He came through an acquaintance who had heard the good news. He proved to be a devil-may-care young fellow whose parents could not make out whether he wanted to stop drinking or not. They were deeply religious people, much shocked by their son's refusal to have anything to do with the church. He suffered horribly from his sprees, but it seemed as if nothing could be done for him. He consented, however, to go to the hospital, where he occupied the very room recently vacated by the lawyer.

He had three visitors. After a bit, he said, "The way you fellows put this spiritual stuff makes sense. I'm ready to do business. I guess the old folks were right after all." So one more was added to the Fellowship.

All this time our friend of the hotel lobby incident remained in that town. He was there three months. He now returned home, leaving behind his first acquaintance, the lawyer and the devil-may-care chap. These men had found something brand new in life. Though they knew they must help other alcoholics if they would remain sober, that motive became secondary. It was transcended by the happiness they found in giving themselves for others. They shared their homes, their slender resources, and gladly devoted their spare hours to fellow-sufferers. They were willing, by day or night, to place a new man in the hospital and visit him afterward. They grew in numbers. They experienced a few distressing failures, but in those cases they made an effort to bring the man's family into a spiritual way of living, thus relieving much worry and suffering.

A year and six months later these three had succeeded with seven more. Seeing much of each other, scarce an evening passed that someone's home did not shelter a little gathering of men and women, happy in their release, and constantly thinking how they might present their discovery to some newcomer. In addition to these casual get-togethers, it became customary to set apart one night a week for a meeting to be attended by anyone or everyone interested in a spiritual way of life. Aside from fellowship and sociability, the prime object was to provide a time and place where new people might bring their problems.

Outsiders became interested. One man and his wife placed their large home at the disposal of this strangely assorted crowd. This couple has since become so fascinated that they have dedicated their home to the work. Many a distracted wife has visited this house to find loving and understanding companionship among women who knew her problem, to hear from the lips of their husbands what had happened to them, to be advised how her own wayward mate might be hospitalized and approached when next he stumbled.

Many a man, yet dazed from his hospital experience, has stepped over the threshold of that home into freedom. Many an alcoholic who entered there came away with an answer. He succumbed to that gay crowd inside, who laughed at their own misfortunes and understood his. Impressed by those who visited him at the hospital, he capitulated entirely when, later, in an upper room of this house, he heard the story of some man whose experience closely tallied with his own. The expression on the faces of the women, that indefinable something in the eyes of the men, the stimulating and electric atmosphere of the place, conspired to let him know that here was haven at last.

The very practical approach to his problems, the absence of intolerance of any kind, the informality, the genuine democracy, the uncanny understanding which these people had were irresistible. He and his wife would leave elated by the thought of what they could now do for some stricken acquaintance and his family. They knew they had a host of new friends; it seemed they had known these strangers always. They had seen miracles, and one was to come to them. They had visioned the Great Reality—their loving and All Powerful Creator.

Now, this house will hardly accommodate its weekly visitors, for they number sixty or eighty as a rule. Alcoholics are being attracted from far and near. From surrounding towns, families drive long distances to be present. A community thirty miles away has fifteen fellows of Alcoholics Anonymous. Being a large place, we think that some day its Fellowship will number many hundreds.*

But life among Alcoholics Anonymous is more than attending gatherings and visiting hospitals. Cleaning up old scrapes, helping to settle family differences, explaining the disinherited son to his irate parents, lending money and securing jobs for each other, when justified—these are everyday occurrences. No one is too discredited or has sunk too low to be welcomed cordially—if he means business. Social distinctions, petty rivalries and jealousies—these are laughed out of countenance. Being wrecked in the same vessel, being restored and united under one God, with hearts and minds attuned to the welfare of others, the things which matter so much to some people no longer signify much to them. How could they?

Under only slightly different conditions, the same thing is taking place in many eastern cities. In one of

* Written in 1939.

these there is a well-known hospital for the treatment of alcoholic and drug addiction. Six years ago one of our number was a patient there. Many of us have felt, for the first time, the Presence and Power of God within its walls. We are greatly indebted to the doctor in attendance there, for he, although it might prejudice his own work, has told us of his belief in ours.

Every few days this doctor suggests our approach to one of his patients. Understanding our work, he can do this with an eye to selecting those who are willing and able to recover on a spiritual basis. Many of us, former patients, go there to help. Then, in this eastern city, there are informal meetings such as we have described to you, where you may now see scores of members. There are the same fast friendships, there is the same helpfulness to one another as you find among our western friends. There is a good bit of travel between East and West and we foresee a great increase in this helpful interchange.

Some day we hope that every alcoholic who journeys will find a Fellowship of Alcoholics Anonymous at his destination. To some extent this is already true. Some of us are salesmen and go about. Little clusters of twos and threes and fives of us have sprung up in other communities, through contact with our two larger centers. Those of us who travel drop in as often as we can. This practice enables us to lend a hand, at the same time avoiding certain alluring distractions of the road, about which any traveling man can inform you.*

Thus we grow. And so can you, though you be but

---

* Written in 1939. In 1993 there were over 89,000 groups. There is A.A. activity in 141 countries, with an estimated membership of two million.

one man with this book in your hand. We believe and hope it contains all you will need to begin.

We know what you are thinking. You are saying to yourself: "I'm jittery and alone. I couldn't do that." But you can. You forget that you have just now tapped a source of power much greater than yourself. To duplicate, with such backing, what we have accomplished is only a matter of willingness, patience and labor.

We know of an A.A. member who was living in a large community. He had lived there but a few weeks when he found that the place probably contained more alcoholics per square mile than any city in the country. This was only a few days ago at this writing. (1939) The authorities were much concerned. He got in touch with a prominent psychiatrist who had undertaken certain responsibilities for the mental health of the community. The doctor proved to be able and exceedingly anxious to adopt any workable method of handling the situation. So he inquired, what did our friend have on the ball?

Our friend proceeded to tell him. And with such good effect that the doctor agreed to a test among his patients and certain other alcoholics from a clinic which he attends. Arrangements were also made with the chief psychiatrist of a large public hospital to select still others from the stream of misery which flows through that institution.

So our fellow worker will soon have friends galore. Some of them may sink and perhaps never get up, but if our experience is a criterion, more than half of those approached will become fellows of Alcoholics Anonymous. When a few men in this city have found themselves, and have discovered the joy of helping others to face life again, there will be no stopping until everyone in that town has had his opportunity to recover—if he can and will.

Still you may say: "But I will not have the benefit of contact with you who write this book." We cannot be sure. God will determine that, so you must remember that your real reliance is always upon Him. He will show you how to create the fellowship you crave.*

Our book is meant to be suggestive only. We realize we know only a little. God will constantly disclose more to you and to us. Ask Him in your morning meditation what you can do each day for the man who is still sick. The answers will come, if your own house is in order. But obviously you cannot transmit something you haven't got. See to it that your relationship with Him is right, and great events will come to pass for you and countless others. This is the Great Fact for us.

Abandon yourself to God as you understand God. Admit your faults to Him and to your fellows. Clear away the wreckage of your past. Give freely of what you find and join us. We shall be with you in the Fellowship of the Spirit, and you will surely meet some of us as you trudge the Road of Happy Destiny.

May God bless you and keep you—until then.

---

* Alcoholics Anonymous will be glad to hear from you.
 Address: P.O. Box 459, Grand Central Station, New York, NY 10163.

DOCTOR BOB'S NIGHTMARE

A co-founder of Alcoholics Anonymous. The birth of our Society dates from his first day of permanent sobriety, June 10, 1935. To 1950, the year of his death, he carried the A.A. message to more than 5,000 alcoholic men and women, and to all these he gave his medical services without thought of charge. In this prodigy of service, he was well assisted by Sister Ignatia at St. Thomas Hospital in Akron, Ohio, one of the greatest friends our Fellowship will ever know.

I WAS BORN in a small New England village of about seven thousand souls. The general moral standard was, as I recall it, far above the average. No beer or liquor was sold in the neighborhood, except at the State liquor agency where perhaps one might procure a pint if he could convince the agent that he really needed it. Without this proof the expectant purchaser would be forced to depart empty handed with none of what I later came to believe was the great panacea for all human ills. Men who had liquor shipped in from Boston or New York by express were looked upon with great distrust and disfavor by most of the good townspeople. The town was well supplied with churches and schools in which I pursued my early educational activities.

My father was a professional man of recognized ability and both my father and mother were most active in church affairs. Both father and mother were considerably above the average in intelligence.

Unfortunately for me, I was the only child, which perhaps engendered the selfishness which played such an important part in bringing on my alcoholism.

From childhood through high school I was more or less forced to go to church, Sunday School and evening service, Monday night Christian Endeavor and sometimes to Wednesday evening prayer meeting. This had the effect of making me resolve that when I was free from parental domination, I would never again darken the doors of a church. This resolution I kept steadfastly for the next forty years, except when circumstances made it seem unwise to absent myself.

After high school came four years in one of the best colleges in the country where drinking seemed to be a major extra-curricular activity. Almost everyone seemed to do it. I did it more and more, and had lots of fun without much grief, either physical or financial. I seemed to be able to snap back the next morning better than most of my fellow drinkers, who were cursed (or perhaps blessed) with a great deal of morning-after nausea. Never once in my life have I had a headache, which fact leads me to believe that I was an alcoholic almost from the start. My whole life seemed to be centered around doing what I wanted to do, without regard for the rights, wishes, or privileges of anyone else; a state of mind which became more and more predominant as the years passed. I was graduated "summa cum laude" in the eyes of the drinking fraternity, but not in the eyes of the Dean.

The next three years I spent in Boston, Chicago, and Montreal in the employ of a large manufacturing concern, selling railway supplies, gas engines of all sorts, and many other items of heavy hardware. During these years, I drank as much as my purse permitted, still without paying too great a penalty, although I was beginning to have morning jitters at times. I lost only a half day's work during these three years.

My next move was to take up the study of medicine, entering one of the largest universities in the country. There I took up the business of drinking with much greater earnestness than I had previously shown. On account of my enormous capacity for beer, I was elected to membership in one of the drinking societies, and soon became one of the leading spirits. Many mornings I have gone to classes, and even though fully prepared, would turn and walk back to the fraternity house because of my jitters, not daring to enter the classroom for fear of making a scene should I be called on for recitation.

This went from bad to worse until Sophomore spring when, after a prolonged period of drinking, I made up my mind that I could not complete my course, so I packed my grip and went South to spend a month on a large farm owned by a friend of mine. When I got the fog out of my brain, I decided that quitting school was very foolish and that I had better return and continue my work. When I reached school, I discovered the faculty had other ideas on the subject. After much argument they allowed me to return and take my exams, all of which I passed creditably. But they were much disgusted and told me they would attempt to struggle along without my presence. After many painful discussions, they finally gave me my credits and I migrated to another of the leading universities of the country and entered as a Junior that fall.

There my drinking became so much worse that the boys in the fraternity house where I lived felt forced to send for my father, who made a long journey in the vain endeavor to get me straightened around. This had little effect however for I kept on drinking and used a great deal more hard liquor than in former years.

Coming up to final exams I went on a particularly strenuous spree. When I went in to write the examinations, my hand trembled so I could not hold a pencil. I passed in at least three absolutely blank books. I was, of course, soon on the carpet and the upshot was that I had to go back for two more quarters and remain absolutely dry, if I wished to graduate. This I did, and proved myself satisfactory to the faculty, both in deportment and scholastically.

I conducted myself so creditably that I was able to secure a much coveted internship in a western city, where I spent two years. During these two years I was kept so busy that I hardly left the hospital at all. Consequently, I could not get into any trouble.

When those two years were up, I opened an office downtown. I had some money, all the time in the world, and considerable stomach trouble. I soon discovered that a couple of drinks would alleviate my gastric distress, at least for a few hours at a time, so it was not at all difficult for me to return to my former excessive indulgence.

By this time I was beginning to pay very dearly physically and, in hope of relief, voluntarily incarcerated myself at least a dozen times in one of the local sanitariums. I was between Scylla and Charybdis now, because if I did not drink my stomach tortured me, and if I did, my nerves did the same thing. After three years of this, I wound up in the local hospital where they attempted to help me, but I would get my friends to smuggle me a quart, or I would steal the alcohol about the building, so that I got rapidly worse.

Finally my father had to send a doctor out from my home town who managed to get me back there in some way, and I was in bed about two months before I could venture out of the house. I stayed about town a couple of months more and then returned to resume my practice. I think I must have been thoroughly scared by what had happened, or by the doctor, or probably both, so that I did not touch a drink again until the country went dry.

With the passing of the Eighteenth Amendment I felt quite safe. I knew everyone would buy a few bottles, or cases, of liquor as their exchequers permitted, and that it would soon be gone. Therefore it would make no great difference, even if I should do some drinking. At that time I was not aware of the almost unlimited supply the government made it possible for us doctors to obtain, neither had I any knowledge of the bootlegger who soon appeared on the horizon. I drank with moderation at first, but it took me only a relatively short time to drift back into the old habits which had wound up so disastrously before.

During the next few years, I developed two distinct phobias. One was the fear of not sleeping, and the other was the fear of running out of liquor. Not being a man of means, I knew that if I did not stay sober enough to earn money, I would run out of liquor. Most of the time, therefore, I did not take the morning drink which I craved so badly, but instead would fill up on large doses of sedatives to quiet the jitters, which distressed me terribly. Occasionally, I would yield to the morning craving, but if I did, it would be only a few hours before I would be quite unfit for work. This would lessen my chances of smuggling some home that evening, which in turn would mean a night of futile tossing around in bed followed by a morning of unbearable jitters. During the subsequent fifteen years I had sense enough never to go to the hospital if I had been drinking, and very seldom did I receive patients. I would sometimes hide out in one of the clubs of which I was a member, and had the habit at times of registering at a hotel under a fictitious name. But my friends usually found me and I would go home if they promised that I should not be scolded.

If my wife was planning to go out in the afternoon, I would get a large supply of liquor and smuggle it home and hide it in the coal bin, the clothes chute, over door jambs, over beams in the cellar and in cracks in the cellar tile. I also made use of old trunks and chests, the old can container, and even the ash container. The water tank on the toilet I never used, because that looked too easy. I found out later that my wife inspected it frequently. I used to put eight or twelve ounce bottles of alcohol in a fur lined glove and toss it onto the back airing porch when winter days got dark enough. My bootlegger had hidden alcohol at the back steps where I could get it at my convenience. Sometimes I would bring it in my pockets, but they were inspected, and that became too risky. I used also to put it up in four ounce bottles and stick several in my stocking tops. This worked nicely until my wife and I went to see Wallace Beery in "Tugboat Annie," after which the pant-leg and stocking racket were out!

I will not take space to relate all my hospital or sanitarium experiences.

During all this time we became more or less ostracized by our friends. We could not be invited out because I would surely get tight and my wife dared not invite people in for the same reason. My phobia for sleeplessness demanded that I get drunk every night, but in order to get more liquor for the next night, I had to stay sober during the day, at least up to four o'clock. This routine went on with few interruptions for seventeen years. It was really a horrible nightmare, this earning money, getting liquor, smuggling it home, getting drunk, morning jitters, taking large doses of sedatives to make it possible for me to earn more money, and so on ad nauseam. I used to promise my wife, my friends, and my children that I would drink no more — promises which seldom kept me sober even through the day, though I was very sincere when I made them.

For the benefit of those experimentally inclined, I should mention the so-called beer experiment. When beer first came back, I thought that I was safe. I could drink all I wanted of that. It was harmless; nobody ever got drunk on beer. So I filled the cellar full, with the permission of my good wife. It was not long before I was drinking at least a case and a half a day. I put on thirty pounds of weight in about two months, looked like a pig, and was uncomfortable from shortness of breath. It then occurred to me that after one was all smelled up with beer nobody could tell what had been drunk, so I began to fortify my beer with straight alcohol. Of course, the result was very bad, and that ended the beer experiment.

About the time of the beer experiment I was thrown in with a crowd of people who attracted me because of their seeming poise, health, and happiness. They spoke with great freedom from embarrassment, which I could never do, and they seemed very much at ease on all occasions and appeared very healthy. More than these attributes, they seemed to be happy. I was self conscious and ill at ease most of the time, my health was at the breaking point, and I was thoroughly miserable. I sensed they had something I did not have, from which I might readily profit. I learned that it was something of a spiritual nature, which did not appeal to me very much, but I thought it could do no harm. I gave the matter much time and study for the next two and a half years, but still got tight every night nevertheless. I read everything I could find, and talked to everyone who I thought knew anything about it.

My wife became deeply interested and it was her interest that sustained mine, though I at no time sensed that it might be an answer to my liquor problem. How my wife kept her faith and courage during all those years, I'll never know, but she did. If she had not, I know I would have been dead a long time ago. For some reason, we alcoholics seem to have the gift of picking out the world's finest women. Why they should be subjected to the tortures we inflict upon them, I cannot explain.

About this time a lady called up my wife one Saturday afternoon, saying she wanted me to come over that evening to meet a friend of hers who might help me. It was the day before Mother's Day and I had come home plastered, carrying a big potted plant which I set down on the table and forthwith went upstairs and passed out. The next day she called again. Wishing to be polite, though I felt very badly, I said, "Let's make the call," and extracted from my wife a promise that we would not stay over fifteen minutes.

We entered her house at exactly five o'clock and it was eleven fifteen when we left. I had a couple of shorter talks with this man afterward, and stopped drinking abruptly. This dry spell lasted for about three weeks; then I went to Atlantic City to attend several days' meeting of a national society of which I was a member. I drank all the scotch they had on the train and bought several quarts on my way to the hotel. This was on Sunday. I got tight that night, stayed sober Monday till after the dinner and then proceeded to get tight again. I drank all I dared in the bar, and then went to my room to finish the job. Tuesday I started in the morning, getting well organized by noon. I did not want to disgrace myself so I then checked out. I bought some more liquor on the way to the depot. I had to wait some time for the train. I remember nothing from then on until I woke up at a friend's house, in a town near home. These good people notified my wife, who sent my newly made friend over to get me. He came and got me home and to bed, gave me a few drinks that night, and one bottle of beer the next morning.

That was June 10, 1935, and that was my last drink. As I write nearly four years have passed.

The question which might naturally come into your mind would be: "What did the man do or say that was different from what others had done or said?" It must be remembered that I had read a great deal and talked to everyone who knew, or thought they knew anything about the subject of alcoholism. But this was a man who had experienced many years of frightful drinking, who had had most all the drunkard's experiences known to man, but who had been cured by the very means I had been trying to employ, that is to say the spiritual approach. He gave me information about the subject of alcoholism which was undoubtedly helpful. *Of far more importance was the fact that he was the first living human with whom I had ever talked, who knew what he was talking about in regard to alcoholism from actual experience. In other words, he talked my language.* He knew all the answers, and certainly not because he had picked them up in his reading.

It is a most wonderful blessing to be relieved of the terrible curse with which I was afflicted. My health is good and I have regained my self-respect and the respect of my colleagues. My home life is ideal and my business is as good as can be expected in these uncertain times.

I spend a great deal of time passing on what I learned to others who want and need it badly. I do it for four reasons:

1. Sense of duty.
2. It is a pleasure.
3. Because in so doing I am paying my debt to the man who took time to pass it on to me.
4. Because every time I do it I take out a little more insurance for myself against a possible slip.

Unlike most of our crowd, I did not get over my craving for liquor much during the first two and one-half years of abstinence. It was almost always with me. But at no time have I been anywhere near yielding. I used to get terribly upset when I saw my friends drink and knew I could not, but I schooled myself to believe that though I once had the same privilege, I had abused it so frightfully that it was withdrawn. So it doesn't behoove me to squawk about it for, after all, nobody ever had to throw me down and pour liquor down my throat.

If you think you are an atheist, an agnostic, a skeptic, or have any other form of intellectual pride which keeps you from accepting what is in this book, I feel sorry for you. If you still think you are strong enough to beat the game alone, that is your affair. But if you really and truly want to quit drinking liquor for good and all, and sincerely feel that you must have some help, we know that we have an answer for you. It never fails, if you go about it with one half the zeal you have been in the habit of showing when you were getting another drink.

Your Heavenly Father will never let you down!

SPIRITUAL EXPERIENCE

The terms "spiritual experience" and "spiritual awakening" are used many times in this book which, upon careful reading, shows that the personality change sufficient to bring about recovery from alcoholism has manifested itself among us in many different forms.

Yet it is true that our first printing gave many readers the impression that these personality changes, or religious experiences, must be in the nature of sudden and spectacular upheavals. Happily for everyone, this conclusion is erroneous.

In the first few chapters a number of sudden revolutionary changes are described. Though it was not our intention to create such an impression, many alcoholics have nevertheless concluded that in order to recover they must acquire an immediate and overwhelming "God-consciousness" followed at once by a vast change in feeling and outlook.

Among our rapidly growing membership of thousands of alcoholics such transformations, though frequent, are by no means the rule. Most of our experiences are what the psychologist William James calls the "educational variety" because they develop slowly over a period of time. Quite often friends of the newcomer are aware of the difference long before he is himself. He finally realizes that he has undergone a profound alteration in his reaction to life; that such a change could hardly have been brought about by himself alone. What often takes place in a few months could seldom have been accomplished by years of self discipline. With few exceptions our members find that they have tapped an unsuspected inner resource which they presently identify with their own conception of a Power greater than themselves.

Most of us think this awareness of a Power greater than ourselves is the essence of spiritual experience. Our more religious members call it "God-consciousness."

Most emphatically we wish to say that any alcoholic capable of honestly facing his problems in the light of our experience can recover, provided he does not close his mind to all spiritual concepts. He can only be defeated by an attitude of intolerance or belligerent denial.

We find that no one need have difficulty with the spirituality of the program. *Willingness, honesty and open mindedness are the essentials of recovery. But these are indispensable.*

"There is a principle which is a bar against all information, which is proof against all arguments and which cannot fail to keep a man in everlasting ignorance— that principle is contempt prior to investigation."

—HERBERT SPENCER

The following is the fifth chapter, "How It Works", from the Original Manuscript of Alcoholics Anonymous. It was this version that was distributed to friends and colleagues of The Fellowship's founders to get comments and suggestions on what to change before sending it to the printer.

ORIGINAL MANUSCRIPT - 1938

Rarely have we seen a person fail who has thoroughly followed our directions. Those who do not recover are people who cannot or will not completely give themselves to this simple program, usually men and women who are constitutionally incapable of being honest with themselves. There are such unfortunates. They are not at fault; they seem to have been born that way. They are naturally incapable of grasping and developing a way of life which demands rigorous honesty. Their chances are less than average. There are those, too, who suffer from grave emotional and mental disorders, but many of them do recover if they have the capacity to be honest.

Our stories disclose in a general way what we used to be like, what happened, and what we are like now. If you have decided you want what we have and are willing to go to any length to get it — then you are ready to follow directions.

At some of these you may balk. You may think you can find an easier, softer way. We doubt if you can. With all the earnestness at our command, we beg of you to be fearless and thorough from the very start. Some of us have tried to hold on to our old ideas and the result was nil until we let go absolutely.

Remember that you are dealing with alcohol — cunning, bafffling, powerful! Without help it is too much for you. But there is One who has all power — That One is God. You must find Him now!

Half measures will avail you nothing. You stand at the turning point. Throw yourself under His protection and care with complete abandon.

Now we think you can take it! Here are the steps we took, which are suggested as your Program of Recovery:

1. Admitted we were powerless over alcohol — that our lives had become unmanageable.
2. Came to believe that a Power greater than ourselves could restore us to sanity.
3. Made a decision to turn our will and our lives over to the care and direction of God as we understood Him.
4. Made a searching and fearless moral inventory of ourselves.
5. Admitted to God, to ourselves, and to another human being the exact nature of our wrongs.
6. Were entirely willing that God remove all these defects of character.
7. Humbly, on our knees, asked Him to remove our shortcomings — holding nothing back.
8. Made a list of all persons we had harmed, and became willing to make complete amends to them all.
9. Made direct amends to such people wherever possible, except when to do so would injure them or others.
10. Continued to take personal inventory and when we were wrong promptly admitted it.
11. Sought through prayer and meditation to improve our contact with God, praying only for knowledge of His will for us and the power to carry that out.

12. Having had a spiritual experience as the result of this
     course of action, we tried to carry this message to oth-
     ers, especially alcoholics, and to practice these prin-
     ciples in all our affairs.

You may exclaim, "What an order! I can't go through with
it." Do not be discouraged. No one among us has been able to
maintain anything like perfect adherence to these principles.
We are not saints. The point is, that we are willing to grow
along spiritual lines. The principles we have set down are guides
to progress. We claim spiritual progress rather than spiritual
perfection.

Our description of the alcoholic, the chapter to the agnostic,
and our personal adventures before and after, have been de-
signed to sell you three pertinent ideas:

(a) That you are alcoholic and cannot manage your own life.
(b) That probably no human power can relieve your alcohol-
    ism.
(c) That God can and will.

If you are not convinced on these vital issues, you ought to re-
read the book to this point or else throw it away!

If you are convinced, you are now at step three, which is that
you make a decision to turn your will and your life over to God
as you understand Him. Just what do we mean by that, and just
what do we do?

The first requirement is that you see that any life run on self-
will can hardly be a success. On that basis we are almost always
in collision with something or somebody, even though our motives may be good. Most people try to live by self-propulsion.
Each person is like an actor who wants to run the whole show:
is forever trying to arrange the lights, the ballet, the scenery
and the rest of the players in his own way. If

his arrangements would only stay put, if only people would do as he wishes, the show would be great. Everybody, including himself, would be pleased. Life would be wonderful. In trying to make these arrangements our actor may sometimes be quite virtuous. He may be kind, considerate, patient, generous; even modest and self-sacrificing. On the other hand, he may be mean, egotistical, selfish and dishonest. But, as with most humans, he is more likely to have varied traits.

What usually happens? The show doesn't come off very well. He begins to think life doesn't treat him right. He decides to exert himself some more. He becomes, on the next occasion, still more demanding or gracious, as the case may be. Still the play does not suit him. Admitting he may be somewhat at fault, he is sure that other people are more to blame. He becomes angry, indignant, self-pitying. What is his basic trouble? Is he not really a self-seeker even when trying to be kind? Is he not a victim of the delusion that he can wrest satisfaction and happiness out of this world if he only manages well? Is it not evident to all the rest of the players that these are the things he wants? And do not his actions make each of them wish to retaliate, snatching all they can get out of the show? Is he not, even in his best moments, a producer of confusion rather than harmony?

Our actor is self-centered — ego-centric, as people like to call it nowadays. He is like the retired business man who lolls in the Florida sunshine in the winter complaining of the sad state of the nation; the preacher who sighs over the sins of the twentieth century; politicians and reformers who are sure all would be Utopia if the rest of the world would only behave; the outlaw safe cracker who thinks society has wronged him; and the alcoholic who has lost all and is locked up. Whatever their protestations, are not these people mostly concerned with themselves, their resentments, or their self-pity?

Selfishness — self-centeredness! That, we think, is the root of our troubles. Driven by a hundred forms of fear, self-delusion, self-seeking, and self-pity, we step on the toes of our fellows and they retaliate. Sometimes they hurt us, seemingly without provocation, but we invariably find that at some time in the past we have made decisions based on self, which later placed us in a position to be hurt.

So our troubles, we think, are basically of our own making. They arise out of ourselves, and the alcoholic is almost the most extreme example that could be found of self-will run riot, though he usually doesn't think so. Above everything, we alcoholics must be rid of this selfishness. We must, or it kills us! God makes that possible. And there is no way of entirely getting rid of self without Him.

You may have moral and philosophical convictions galore, but you can't live up to them even though you would like to. Neither can you reduce your self-centeredness much by wishing or trying on your own power. You must have God's help.

This is the how and why of it. First of all, quit playing God yourself. It doesn't work. Next, decide that hereafter in this drama of life, God is going to be your Director. He is the Principal; you are to be His agent. He is the Father, and you are His child. Get that simple relationship straight. Most good ideas are simple and this concept is to be the keystone of the new and triumphant arch through which you will pass to freedom.

When you sincerely take such a position, all sorts of remarkable things follow. You have a new Employer. Being all powerful, He must necessarily provide what you need, if you keep close to Him and perform His work well. Established on such a footing you become less and less interested in yourself, your little plans and designs. More and more you become interested in seeing what you can contribute to life. As you feel new power flow in, as you enjoy peace of mind, as you discover you can face life successfully, and as you become conscious of His presence, you begin to lose your fear of today, tomorrow, or the hereafter. You will have been reborn.

Get down upon your knees and say to your Maker, <u>as you understand Him</u>: "God, I offer myself to Thee — to build with me and to do with me as Thou wilt. Relieve me of the bondage of self, that I may better do Thy will. Take away my difficulties, that victory over them may bear witness to those I would help of Thy Power, Thy Love, and Thy Way of life. May I do Thy will always!" Think well before taking this step. Be sure you are ready; that you can at least abandon yourself utterly to Him.

It is very desirable that you make your decision with an understanding person. It may be your wife, your best friend, your spiritual adviser, but remember it is better to meet God alone that with one who might misunderstand. You must decide this for yourself. The wording of your decision is, of course, quite optional so long as you express the idea, voicing it without reservation. This decision is only a beginning, though if honestly and humbly made, an effect, sometimes a very great one, will be felt at once.

Next we launch out on a course of vigorous action, the first step of which is a personal housecleaning, which you have never in all probability attempted. Though your decision is a vital and crucial step, it can have little permanent effect unless at once followed by a strenuous effort to face, and to be rid of, the things in yourself which have been blocking you. Your liquor is but a symptom. Let's now get down to basic causes and conditions.

Therefore, you start upon a personal inventory. This is step four. A business which takes no regular inventory usually goes broke. Taking a commercial inventory is a fact-finding and fact-facing process. It is an effort to discover the truth about the stock in trade. Its object is to disclose damaged or unsalable goods, to get rid of them promptly and without regret. If the owner of the business is to be successful, he cannot fool himself about values.

We do exactly the same thing with our lives. We take stock honestly. First, we search out the flaws in our make-up which have caused our failure. Being convinced that self, manifested in various ways, is what has defeated us, we consider its common manifestations.

Resentment is the "number one" offender. It destroys more alcoholics than anything else. From it stem all forms of spiritual disease, for we have been not only mentally and physically ill, we have been spiritually sick. When the spiritual malady is overcome, we straighten out mentally and physically. In dealing with resentments, we set them on paper. List people, institutions or principles with whom you are angry. Ask yourself why you are angry. In most cases it will be found that your self-esteem, your pocketbook, your ambitions, your personal relationships (including sex) are hurt or threatened. So you are sore. You are "burned up."

On your grudge list set opposite each name your injuries. Is it your self-esteem, your security, your ambitions, your personal, or your sex relations, which have been interfered with?

Be as definite as this example:

I'm resentful at:	The Cause	Affects my:
Mr. Brown	His attention to my wife.	Sex relations. Self-esteem (fear)
	Told my wife of my mistress.	Sex relations. Self-esteem (fear)
	Brown may get my job at the office.	Security. Self-esteem (fear)
Mrs. Jones	She's a nut -- she snubbed me. She committed her husband for drinking. He's my friend. She's a gossip.	Personal relationship. Self-esteem (fear)
My employer	Unreasonable - Unjust - Overbearing - Threatens to fire me for drinking and padding my expense account.	Self-esteem (fear) Security
My wife	Misunderstands and nags. Likes Brown. Wants house put in her name.	Pride - Personal and sex relations - Security (fear)

Go on through the list back through your lifetime. Nothing counts but thoroughness and honesty. When you are finished consider it carefully.

The first thing apparent to you is that this world and its people are often quite wrong. To conclude that others are wrong is as far as most of us ever get. The usual outcome is that people continue to wrong you and you stay sore. Sometimes it is remorse and then you are sore at yourself. But the more you fight and try to have your way, the worse matters get. Isn't that so? As in war, victors only <u>seem</u> to win. Your moments of triumph are short-lived.

It is plain that a way of life which includes deep resentment leads only to futility and unhappiness. To the precise extent that we permit these, do we squander the hours that might have been worth while. But with the alcoholic whose only hope is the maintenance and growth of a spiritual experience, this business of resentment is infinitely grave. We find that it is fatal. For when harboring such feelings we shut ourselves off from the sunlight of the Spirit. The insanity of alcohol returns and we drink again. And with us, to drink is to die.

If we are to live, we must be free of anger. The grouch and the brainstorm are not for us. They may be the dubious luxury of normal men, but for alcoholics these things are poison.

Turn back to your list, for it holds the key to your future. You must be prepared to look at it from an entirely different angle. You will begin to see that the world and its people really dominate you. In your present state, the wrongdoing of others, fancied or real, has power to actually kill you. How shall you escape? You see that these resentments must be mastered, but how? You cannot wish them away any more than alcohol.

This is our course: realize at once that the people who wronged you are spiritually sick.

Though you don't like their symptoms and the way these disturb you, they, like yourself, are sick, too. Ask God to help you show them the same tolerance, pity, and patience that you would cheerfully grant a friend who has cancer. When a person next offends, say to yourself "This is a sick man. How can I be helpful to him? God save me from being angry. Thy will be done."

Never argue. Never retaliate. You wouldn't treat sick people that way. If you do, you destroy your chance of being helpful. You cannot be helpful to all people, but at least God will show you how to take a kindly and tolerant view of each and every one.

Take up your list again. Putting out of your mind the wrongs others have done, resolutely look for your own mistakes. Where have you been selfish, dishonest, self-seeking and frightened? Though a situation may not be entirely your fault, disregard the other person involved entirely. See where you have been to blame. This is your inventory, not the other man's. When you see your fault write it down on the list. See it before you in black and white. Admit your wrongs honestly and be willing to set these matters straight.

You will notice that the word fear is bracketed alongside the difficulties with Mr. Brown, Mrs. Jones, your employer, and your wife. This short word somehow touches about every aspect of our lives. It is an evil and corroding thread; the fabric of our existence is shot through with it. It sets in motion trains of circumstances which bring us misfortune we feel we don't deserve. But did not we, ourselves, set the ball rolling? Sometimes we think fear ought to be classed with stealing as a sin. It seems to cause more trouble.

Review your fears thoroughly. Put them on paper, even though you have no resentment in connection with them. Ask yourself why you have them. Isn't it because self-reliance has failed you? Self-reliance was good as far as it went, but it didn't go far enough. Some of us once had great self-confidence, but it didn't fully solve the fear problem, or any other. When it made us cocky, it was worse.

Perhaps there is a better way — we think so. For you are now to go on a different basis; the basis of trusting and relying upon God. You are to trust infinite God rather than your finite self. You are in the world to play the role he assigns. Just to the extent that you do as you think He would have you, and humbly rely on Him, does He enable you to match calamity with serenity.

You must never apologize to anyone for depending upon your Creator. You can laugh at those who think spirituality the way of weakness. Paradoxically, it is the way of strength. The verdict of the ages is that faith means courage. All men of faith have courage. They trust their God. Never apologize for God. Instead let Him demonstrate, through you, what He can do. Ask Him to remove your fear and direct your attention to what He would have you be. At once, you will commence to outgrow fear.

Now about sex. You can probably stand an overhauling there. We needed it. But above all, let's be sensible on this question. It's so easy to get way off the track. Here we find human opinions running to extremes — absurd extremes, perhaps. One set of voices cry that sex is a lust of our lower nature, a base necessity of procreation. Then we have the voices who cry for sex and more sex; who bewail the institution of marriage; who think that most of the troubles of the race are traceable to sex causes. They think we do not have enough of it, or that it isn't the right kind. They see its significance everywhere. One school would allow man no flavor for his fare and the other would have us all on a straight pepper diet. We want to stay out of this controversy. We do not want to be the arbiter of anyone's sex conduct. We all have sex problems. We'd hardly be human if we didn't. What can we do about them?

Review your own conduct over the years past. Where have you been selfish, dishonest, or inconsiderate? Whom did you hurt? Did you unjustifiably arouse jealousy, suspicion or bitterness? Where you were at fault, what should you have done instead? Get this all down on paper and look at it.

In this way you can shape a sane and sound ideal for your future sex life. Subject each relation to this test — is it selfish or not? Ask God to mold your ideals and help you to live up to them. Remember always that your sex powers are God-given, and therefore good, neither to be used lightly or selfishly nor to be despised and loathed.

Whatever your ideal may be, you must be willing to grow toward it. You must be willing to make amends where you have done harm, provided that you will not bring about still more harm in so doing. In other words, treat sex as you would any other problem. In meditation, ask God what you should do about each specific matter. The right answer will come, if you want it.

God alone can judge your sex situation. Counsel with

persons is often desirable, but let God be the final judge. Remember that some people are as fanatical about sex as others are loose. Avoid hysterical thinking or advice.

Suppose you fall short of the chosen ideal and stumble. Does this mean you are going to get drunk? Some people will tell you so. If they do, it will be only a half-truth. It depends on you and your motive. If you are sorry for what you have done, and have the honest desire to let God take you to better things, you will be forgiven and will have learned your lesson. If you are not sorry, and your conduct continues to harm others, you are quite sure to drink. We are not theorizing. These are facts out of our experience.

To sum up about sex: earnestly pray for the right ideal, for guidance in each questionable situation, for sanity, and for the strength to do the right thing. If sex is very troublesome, throw yourself the harder into helping others. Think of their needs and work for them. This will take you out of yourself. It will quiet the imperious urge, when to yield would mean heartache.

If you have been thorough about your personal inventory, you have written down a lot by this time. You have listed and analyzed your resentments. You have begun to comprehend their futility and their fatality. You have commenced to see their terrible destructiveness. You have begun to learn tolerance, patience and good will toward all men, even your enemies, for you know them to be sick people. You have listed the people you have hurt by your conduct, and you are willing to straighten out the past if you can.

In this book you read again and again that God

did for us what we could not do for ourselves. We hope you are convinced now that He can remove the self-will that has blocked you off from Him. You have made your decision. You have made an inventory of the grosser handicaps you have. You have made a good beginning, for you have swallowed and digested some big chunks of truth about yourself. Are you willing to go on?

The "Original Manuscript" of the first 164 pages is available from:

Alcoholics Anonymous World Service, Inc.
P.O. Box 459
Grand Central Station
New York, NY 10163 $12.00

Glad Publications
966 Palmwood Dr.
Sparks, NV 89434 $10.00

Kelly Foundation
2500 S. Broadway
Little Rock, AR 72206
                                                      $8.95
───────

The entire "Original Manuscript", including the stories, is available from:

The Anonymous Press
P.O. Box 1212
Malo WA 99150-1212
(800) 800-4398
Entire text is included in The Workbook Edition. $4.75

– with a side glance; sidewise; obliquely.

– with suspicion or disapproval; skeptically: The company may view askance your plan for early retirement.

Asked 20, 51, 56, 59, 68, 69, 80

Asking 47, 83, 89, 107

Assert 23, 130, 131

Assets 89, 124

Assistance 78, 96, 98, 136

Associates 15, 145

Association 28

Assumed 47, 97, 100, 128

Assuming 34

Assumption 48

Assure xxix, 47, 89, 142

Astonishingly xxvi, 30

Astonishment xviii

Asylum 7, 15, 31, 35, 36, 38, 97

asylum (uh sī'luhm) n.

– (esp. formerly) an institution for the maintenance and care of the mentally ill, orphans, or other persons requiring specialized assistance.

– an inviolable refuge, as formerly for criminals and debtors; sanctuary.

– a. a refuge granted an alien by a sovereign state on its own territory.

b. a temporary refuge granted political offenders, esp. in a foreign embassy.

Atheist 10, 44, 49, 52, 55, 93

atheist (AY'thEE ist) n.

– a person who denies or disbelieves the existence of a supreme being or beings.

Attachment 137

Attempt 33, 94, 111, 125, 151

Attempted 32, 64, 141

Attend 87, 102

Attended xxiii, 56, 80, 141, 161

Attention 1, 23, 65, 68, 90, 93, 107, 119, 143, 144, 149

Attitude 18, 19, 25, 27, 50, 55, 72, 77, 84-86, 99, 103, 117, 122, 143-145, 149, 150

Attractive 39, 154, 161

Attributes 53

Attuned 161

Authority 74, 78, 163

Automatically 85

Avail 24, 59

Available 74, 96, 134

Average xxvi, 17, 43, 58, 129

Avocation xiii

avocation (av'uh kAY'shuhn) n.

– something a person does in addition to a principal occupation, esp. for pleasure; hobby.

– a person's regular occupation or calling; vocation.

– Archaic. diversion or distraction.

Avoid 43, 67, 70, 72, 83, 91, 97, 98, 101, 113-115, 118, 123, 126

Avoided 126

Avoiding 85, 117

Awakening 86, 151

Aware 19, 109, 155

Awe 4, 46

Bad 29, 43, 76, 115, 132, 140

Bad-intentioned 108

Badly 20, 43, 133

Baffling 23, 26, 34, 51, 58, 62, 84, 92, 107

Balance 11, 21, 39, 131

Balked 58

derived from: balk (bôk) v.

– to refuse curtly and firmly (usually followed by at): He balked at making the speech.

– to stop short and stubbornly refuse to go on.

– to commit a balk in baseball.

Balmy 128

balmy (bä'mEE) adj.

– mild and refreshing; soft; soothing: balmy weather.

– Informal. crazy; foolish; eccentric.

Bankruptcy 34

Bar 6, 36, 41, 101

Barroom 31

Barriers 56, 115, 126

Base 68

Based 121, 124

Basic 52, 61

Basically 62

Basis 9, 33, 39, 50, 60, 68, 79, 99, 118, 120, 135, 146

Battle 6, 103

Beating 6

Beauty 50

Became 13, 59

Bed 8, 19, 41, 56, 157

condemn (kuhn dem') v.
- to express an unfavorable or adverse judgment on; indicate strong disapproval of; censure.
- to sentence to punishment, esp. a severe punishment: to condemn a murderer to death.
- to pronounce to be guilty.

Condition xxix, 9, 18, 26, 32, 35, 39, 42, 64, 77, 85, 86, 90, 93, 97, 98, 101, 107, 111, 114, 122, 134, 143, 144

Conduct 38, 70

Confession 25, 74

Confidence 6, 14, 18, 26, 40, 54, 74, 75, 78, 89, 114, 123, 143

Confined 26, 56

Confronted 53

Confused 93

Confusion 61

Conquer 44

Conquering 98

Conscience 95, 132
conscience (kon'shuhns) n.
- the inner sense of what is right or wrong in one's conduct or motives, impelling one toward right action: to follow the dictates of conscience.
- the complex of ethical and moral principles that controls or inhibits the actions or thoughts of an individual.
- an inhibiting sense of what is prudent.

Conscientiously 58
derived from: conscientious (kon'shEE en'shuhs) adj.
- meticulous; careful; painstaking.
- governed by or done according to conscience; scrupulous: a conscientious judge.

Consciousness 24, 25, 51, 55, 59, 63, 98, 130, 147

Consents 80

Consequences 24, 37, 41, 79

Consider 65

Considerably 22, 29, 30, 34, 46, 64, 86

Considerate 61, 99

Consigned 152
derived from: consign (kuhn sIn?) v.
- to hand over or deliver; assign.
- to transfer to another's custody or charge; entrust.
- to banish or set apart; relegate: to

consign unpleasant thoughts to oblivion.

Console 14

Consternation 35
consternation (kon'stuhr nAY'shuhn) n.
- a sudden, alarming amazement or dread that results in utter confusion; dismay.

Constitutionally 58
constitutionally (kon'sti tU'shuh nl EE) adv.
- in respect to physical makeup.
- in respect to mental or emotional makeup: constitutionally shy.
- with respect to a constitution.

Construction 2, 54, 127

Constructive 86, 93

Consult 94, 114, 126

Consulting 80, 134

Consummation 25
derived from: consummate (kon'suh mAYt) v.
- to bring to a state of perfection; fulfill.
- to bring to a state of completion, as an arrangement or agreement.
- to complete (the union of a marriage) by the first marital sexual intercourse.

Consumption 21, 25

Contact 35, 46, 59, 89, 131, 138, 139, 144, 164

Contempt 10

Contention 19, 49, 118

Contingent 85

Continue 3, 38, 44, 59, 66, 70, 92, 96, 97, 99, 111

Contradict 94

Contrary 147

Contribute xxv, 63

Contrition 126
contrition (kuhn trish'uhn) n.
- sincere penitence or remorse.
- sorrow for sin with a true purpose of amendment.

Control xxiv, xxvii, 5, 21, 26, 30-32, 44, 52, 92, 109, 117, 139, 151, 155

Controlled drinking 30, 31, 32

Controversial 19

Controversies 69

Convalescence 129
convalescence (kon'vuh les'uhns) n.
- the gradual recovery of health and

Daily xxvi, 134

Damn 157

Dances 101

Danger xxviii, 88

Dangerous 117, 126

Dangerously 21, 34

Dared 6, 8

Daring 158

Dark 8, 75, 110, 124

Dazed 160

Dead 11, 15, 33, 88, 135

Deadly 16

Deal 5, 23, 58, 64, 78, 90-91, 93, 94, 107, 113, 125, 133, 142, 144, 149

Dealt 18

Death 21, 24, 30, 31, 33, 44, 75, 107, 154

Debacle 22

debacle (duh bä'kuhl) n.
– a disaster or fiasco.
– a general rout or dispersal of troops.
– a breaking up of ice in a river.

Debate xxviii

Debauch 8, 104

debauch (di bôch') v.
– to corrupt (another's virtue or chastity) by sensuality, intemperance, etc.; seduce.
– to subvert (honesty, integrity, or the like).
– Archaic. to corrupt (allegiance, loyalty, or the like).

Decide 28, 32, 36, 38, 41, 58-62, 64, 71, 75, 79, 82, 86, 90, 95, 96, 103, 113, 140, 147

Decision 21

Dedicated 160

Deep 25, 35, 55, 66, 93, 158

Defeat 11, 42, 64, 115

Defeated 153

Defects 50, 59, 72, 83, 99, 100, 118

derived from: defect (dEE fekt) n.
– a fault or shortcoming; imperfection.
– lack of something essential; deficiency: a defect in hearing.

Defects of character 50, 59, 72, 99, 100, 118

Defend 146

Defense 24, 42, 43

Deficiencies 13, 120

Definite xxvi, 32, 65, 87

Deflation 122

Delighted 75

Delinquencies 126

Delirium 13

delirium (di lEEr'EE uhm) n.
– a temporary disturbance of consciousness characterized by restlessness, excitement, and delusions or hallucinations.
– a state of violent excitement or emotion.

Delusion 30, 61

Demands 58, 61, 122, 123, 143

Democracy 17

Demonstrate 14, 19, 25, 33, 49, 55, 68, 77, 98, 99, 133

Demoralization 30

derived from: demoralize (di môr'uh llz') v.
– to deprive (a person or persons) of spirit, courage, discipline, etc.; destroy the morale of.
– to throw (a person) into disorder or confusion; bewilder.
– to corrupt or undermine the morals of.

Denial 10, 20-23, 30, 31

Denied 80

Denizens 151

derived from: denizen (den'uh zuhn) n.
– an inhabitant; resident.
– a person who regularly frequents a place; habitué.
– Brit. an alien admitted to residence and to certain rights of citizenship.

Denomination xiv, 74, 87, 93, 94

Deny 96

Depend 68, 70, 80

Dependable 54

Dependence 46, 98, 100

Deportment 18

deportment (di pôrt'muhnt) n.
– conduct; behavior.

Depression xxix, 37, 39, 52, 56, 106, 127, 153

Depressive xxviii

Deprived 96

Deranged 14

Derelictions 143

derived from: dereliction (der'uh lik'shuhn) n.
– deliberate or conscious neglect;

loath (lowth) adj.
  – hateful; odious.
  – unwilling; reluctant; averse.

longshoreman (long' shore' man) n.
  – a person who works on a waterfront
    loading and unloading ships.

lucid (loo'sid) adj.
  – shining; bright; resplendent.
  – clear; transparent.
  – sane; mentally sound.

lunacy (loo'na see) n.
  – originally, intermittent insanity,
    formerly supposed to change in
    intensity with the phases of the moon.
  – great folly; utter foolishness.

lunar (lU'nuhr) adj.
  – of or pertaining to the moon: the lunar
    orbit.
  – measured by the moon's revolutions:
    a lunar month.
  – resembling the moon; round or
    crescent-shaped.

maelstrom (mAYl'struhm) n.
  – a powerful whirlpool often hazardous
    to approach.
  – a tumultuous state of affairs.
  – a powerful current off the NW coast
    of Norway.

malicious (muh lish'uhs) adj.

the zenith.
– the lowest point; point of greatest adversity or despair.

Napoleon 4
Narrow 158
Nation 61
Natural 31, 53, 118
Naturally 58, 99, 107, 145
Nature 59, 115
Near 8, 57
Nearly 17, 104
Nearness 75
Necessarily 33
Necessary 27, 73, 142
Necessity 19, 34, 74
Need 8, 20, 26, 50, 76, 102, 119, 156
Needed 45, 47, 116
Needless 146
Needlessly 82
Needs 70, 91
Neglect 129
Nervous xxix, 32, 35
Nervousness 37
Neurotic 122

neurotic (noo rot'ik) adj.
– of, pertaining to, or characteristic of neurosis.
– a neurotic person.

Neutrality 85

neutrality (nU tral'i tEE) n.
– the state of being neutral.
– the policy or status of a nation that does not participate in a war between other nations.
– neutral status, as of a seaport during a war.

Never 30, 31, 50, 51, 57, 77, 97, 105, 111, 123, 158
Nevertheless 26, 40, 87
New 11, 14, 28, 46, 50, 52, 83, 126, 131, 134, 135, 161
New England 1
Newcomers 15, 72, 89, 100, 132, 133, 159
New York 9, 41
Night 2, 3, 6, 8, 21, 41, 46, 56, 81, 86, 97, 100, 126, 128, 134
Nightclubs 101
Nightmare 73
Nil 58
Nominal 42

nominal (nom'uh nl) adj.

– being such in name only; so-called; putative: the nominal head of the country.
– (of a price, fee, etc.) named as a matter of form, being trifling in comparison with the actual value: a nominal price.
– of, pertaining to, or constituting a name or names.

Non-alcoholic 31, 39, 44
Non-denominational 132
Non-spiritual 34
Normal xxvi, xxviii, 35, 38, 66, 113
Normal drinker 31, 140
Normally 17, 33
Nothing 19, 25, 40, 41, 49, 53, 54, 59, 65, 75, 79, 89, 91, 105
Now xxvi, xxx, 20, 55, 59, 76, 163
Number 31, 109, 110, 153, 162
Numbers 16, 33
Nurse 95
Nurses 156
Oasis 9

oasis (O AY'sis) n.
– a fertile area in a desert region, usually having a spring or well.
– a refuge, as from work or stress; haven.

Oath 31
Obeyed 131
Obligation 94
Obligations 129
Obliged 115, 125
Oblivion 19
Observations 20, 23
Observe 49, 73
Observed 49, 73
Obsession 23, 30, 155
Obstacles 123
Obstinacy 48

obstinacy (ob'stuh nuh sEE) n.
– the quality or state of being obstinate; stubbornness.
– an instance of being obstinate; an obstinate act, viewpoint, etc.

Obviously 18, 45, 99, 164
Occasion 61, 101, 102, 105, 124
Occasional 87
Occasionally 78, 97, 134
Oddly 110
Offender 64
Offense 78

* Topic is discussed but not directly mentioned on this page.

Promptly xvii, 64

Proof 48

Prophesied 41
derived from: prophesy (prof'uh sI') v.
– to foretell or predict.
– to indicate beforehand.
– to utter in prophecy or as a prophet, esp. by divine inspiration.

Prosaic 48
prosaic (prO zAY'ik) adj.
– commonplace or dull; matter-of-fact; unimaginative; a prosaic mind.
– of or like prose rather than poetry.

Protect 146

Protege 92
protégé (prO'tuh zhAY') n.
– a person under the patronage, protection, or care of someone interested in his or her career or welfare.

Prove xiii, 2, 31, 32, 47, 51, 54, 141

Provided 27, 43, 46, 48, 63, 69, 79, 93, 98, 102, 146, 147, 160

Providence 101
providence (prov'i duhns) n.
– (often cap.) the foreseeing care and guidance of God or nature over the creatures of the earth.
– (cap.) God, esp. when conceived as exercising such care and guidance in directing human affairs.
– a manifestation of divine care or direction.

Provocation 62, 124, 146
provocation (prov'uh kAY'shuhn) n.
– the act of provoking.
– something that provokes, esp. by inciting, instigating, angering, or irritating.

Psychiatric 19
derived from: psychiatry (si kI'uh trEE) n.
– the branch of medicine concerned with the study, diagnosis, and treatment of mental disorders.

Psychiatrists 18, 26, 114, 133, 163

Psychic xxvii

Psychologist 28, 73, 74, 133

Psychology xxv, xxix

Publication xiii

Publicly xiii

Purpose xiii, 10, 50, 77, 92, 130

Qualified 32

Qualities 140

Quarrels 100, 147

Queer 38, 92
queer (kwEEr) adj.
– strange or odd from a conventional viewpoint; unusually different; singular; eccentric.
– of a questionable nature or character; suspicious; shady: something queer in the wording of the document.
– not physically right or well; giddy, faint, or qualmish.

Queried 9
derived from: query (kwEEr'EE) n.
– a question; an inquiry.
– mental reservation; doubt.

Questionable 70

Questions 20, 34, 56, 98, 108

Quicksand 8

Quiet 94

Quit 20, 34, 39, 90, 91, 141

Quitting 34

Rabbi 132
rabbi (rab'I) n.
– the chief religious official of a synagogue who performs ritualistic, educational, and other functions as spiritual leader of the congregation.
– a title of respect for a Jewish scholar or teacher.
– a Jewish scholar qualified to rule on questions of Jewish law.

Races 49

Racket 158

Radically 117, 146

Rancor 111, 134
rancor (rang'kuhr) n.
– bitter resentment or ill will; malice.

Ranting 9

Rarely 58

Reacts 19, 21, 26, 37, 43, 81

Read xxx, 70, 95, 96, 112, 113, 114, 133, 144, 147

Reader xxiii, 27, 34, 48

Readily 48

Readiness 52, 74

Readjustment 122, 146

Ready 58, 59

Real alcoholic 30, 31

Reality xxiv, 50, 55, 130

Real purpose 77

* Topic is discussed but not directly mentioned on this page.

Repel 103

Repetition 120

Replaced 130

Representation 17

Reprieve 85

reprieve (ri prEEv') v.
- to delay the impending punishment or sentence of (a condemned person).
- to relieve temporarily from any evil.
- a respite from impending punishment, esp. from execution.

Reproached 123

derived from: reproach (ri prOch') v.
- to find fault with (a person, group, etc.); blame; censure.
- to criticize severely; upbraid.
- to be a cause of blame or discredit to.

Reproved 126

derived from: reprove (ri prUv') v.
- to criticize or correct, esp. gently.
- to express strong disapproval of; censure.
- to disprove or refute.

Reputation 73, 80, 105, 126

Request xxiv, 13, 87

Requirement 60, 94

Requirements 50

Requires xxvi, xxvii, 12, 50, 72

Resentment 15, 18, 64, 66, 68, 70, 79, 84, 86, 100, 105, 116, 117, 119, 122, 126, 127, 145

Resentful 81

Resentments 62, 100

Reservation 33, 63

Reserve 18, 51

Resign 31, 148

Resist xxix, 12

Resistant 155

Resolutely 84

derived from: resolute (rez'uh lUt') adj.
- firmly set in purpose or opinion; determined; resolved.
- characterized by firmness and determination.

Resolutions xxviii, 34

Resolve 5

Respect xxviii, 19,43

Respective 19, 91

Respond 96

Responsibilities 97, 120, 130, 137, 154

Restless xxvi

Restored 57, 59

Resulting xxvii

Results xiv, 4, 9, 78, 99, 134, 138, 144

Retaliate 61, 62, 67, 105

Retaliation 67, 103

Retired 32, 33, 61

Retreat 129

Revealed 48

Revelation 57

Reverse 114

Review 75, 86

Reviewing 35, 68, 75

Revolutionary 14, 50

Revolutionized 25

Revulsion 5, 7, 141

revulsion (ri vul'shuhn) n.
- a strong feeling of repugnance, distaste, or dislike; disgust; loathing.
- a sudden and violent change of feeling or response in sentiment, taste, etc.
- the act of drawing something back or away.

Rid 62, 64

Ridiculous 38

Right 69, 74, 81, 83, 86, 87, 100

Righteous 152

Rigorous 58, 145

rigorous (rig'uhr uhs) adj.
- characterized by rigid severity: rigorous laws.
- severely exact; precise: rigorous research.
- extremely inclement; harsh: rigorous weather.

Rise 45, 153

Rising 123

Rival 80

Rivalries 161

Road 104, 114, 129, 164

Roaring 82, 155

Robust 33

Rocketed 25

Rough 15, 72

Ruin 101, 107, 108

Ruined 80, 82, 109

Ruinous 80

ruinous (rU'uh nuhs) adj.
- bringing or tending to bring ruin; destructive; disastrous: a ruinous war.
- fallen into ruin; dilapidated.
- extremely expensive.

* Topic is discussed but not directly mentioned on this page.

* Topic is discussed but not directly mentioned on this page.

* Topic is discussed but not directly mentioned on this page.

Subtle 8
subtle (sut'l) adj.
– thin, tenuous, or rarefied, as a fluid or an
  odor.
– fine or delicate in meaning or intent;
  difficult to perceive or understand:
  subtle irony.
– delicate or faint and mysterious: a subtle
  smile.

Succumbed xxviii
derived from: succumb (suh kum') v.
– to give way to superior force; yield.
– to yield to disease, wounds, old age,
  etc.; die.

Suffices xxvi
derived from: suffice (suh fis') v.
– to be enough or adequate, as for
  needs or purposes.
– to be enough or adequate for; satisfy.

Summa cum laude 172
summa cum laude (soom'uh koom
lou'duh) adv.
– with highest praise: used in diplomas
  to grant the highest of three special
  honors for grades above the average.

Sumptuous 3
sumptuous (sump'chU uhs) adj.
– entailing great expense, as from
  choice materials, fine work, etc.;
  cos'ly.
– luxuriously fine or large; lavish;
  splendid: a sumptuous feast.

Supplanted 24
derived from: supplant (suh' plant) v.
– to take the place of (another), as
  through force, scheming, or strategy.
– to replace (one thing) by something
  else.

Tact 77
tact (tacked) n.
– touch; a touching.
– the sense of touch.
– intuitive perception, especially a
  quick and fine perception of the
  proper thing to say or to do to avoid

giving offense.

Tactful 83

Tangent 130

tangent (tan'juhnt) n.
- digressing suddenly from one course of action or thought and turning to another.

Tangible 99

tangible (tan'juh buhl) adj.
- capable of being touched; discernible by touch; material or substantial.
- real or actual, rather than imaginary or visionary.
- definite; not vague or elusive: no tangible grounds for suspicion.

Tedious 48

tedious (tEE'dEE uhs) adj.
- marked by tedium; long and tiresome.
- tiresomely wordy, as a speaker or writer.

Teetotaler 139

Telephone 8, 97

Temper 111

Temperament 108

temperament (tem'puhr uh muhnt) n.
- the combination of mental and emotional traits of a person; natural predisposition.
- unusual personal nature as manifested by peculiarities of feeling, temper, action, etc., often with a disinclination to submit to conventional rules or restraints: a display of temperament.
- (old physiology) the combination of the four cardinal humors, the relative proportions of which were supposed to determine physical and mental constitution.

Temperance 10

temperance (tem'per anse) n.
- self restraint in conduct.
- moderation in eating and drinking.
- total abstinence from alcoholic liquors.

Temporarily 111

Temptation 57, 85, 101, 120, 147, 181

Tendencies 24, 125, 134

Tension 73, 115

Terrible 23, 28, 141

Test 13

Testimony 55

Thanked 155

Theological 93

Theorizing 70

Theory 52

Think 24, 62, 68, 69, 126

Thinking 13, 24, 35, 37, 48, 50, 53, 70, 74, 86, 87, 114, 118, 158

Thorough 58, 62, 70

Thoroughly 58

Thoroughness 63

Thought 63

Thoughtful 123

Thought-Life 86

Threadbare 24

threadbare (thred'bâr) adj.
- having the nap worn off so as to lay bare the threads of the weave, as a fabric or garment.
- wearing threadbare clothes; shabby or poor.
- hackneyed; trite; ineffectively stale: threadbare arguments.

Threshold 41, 160

Thy will be done 88

Tight 21, 115

Tolerance 19, 67, 70, 83, 84, 118, 122, 125, 127, 138

Tomorrow 63

Tornado 82

Track 68, 100

Tragedies xxvi

Tragic 16, 21, 23, 24

Traits 92

Transcended 159

Transformation 133, 143

Traveling 49, 52, 104, 162

Treat 61, 67, 108, 129

Treatment xxiii, xxix, 13, 26, 30, 142, 143, 148, 157

Trembling 8, 73, 115

Tremendous 17

Tried 60, 66-68, 72

Trifle 126

trifle (trI'fuhl) n.
- something of very little value, importance, or consequence.
- a small, inconsiderable, or trifling amount of anything.
- a dessert of cake soaked in liqueur, then combined with custard, fruit, jam, etc., and topped with whipped cream.

* Topic is discussed but not directly mentioned on this page.

The Anonymous Press
welcomes suggestions for
changes to this index.

Index Committee
The Anonymous Press
PO Box 1212
Malo, WA 99150
USA

This Index is also available on
The Internet at:
http://www.recovery.org/aa
This site is not run by
The Anonymous Press, but we
contribute to it as a service to our
fellows.

* Topic is discussed but not directly mentioned on this page.

Additions and Corrections

For corrections to this directory, please call us at (800) 800-4398.
Please use this number **_ONLY_** to report corrections, additions or to order these books.
The Anonymous Press is not endorsed by, or affiliated with, those listed below.
Up-to-date listings can be found on The Internet at: http://www.recovery.org/aa
(This site is not run by The Anonymous Press)

WORLDWIDE		
INTERNET	http://aa-intergroup.org	

ALABAMA		
ALBERTVILLE	(205)878-8140
ALEXANDER CITY	(205)329-9373
ARAB	(205)586-6621
ATHENS	(205)232-6410
BESSEMER	(205)428-7021
BIRMINGHAM	(205)933-8964
CULLMAN	(205)739-1443
DECATUR	(205)350-1544
DOTHAN	(334)792-1759
HUNTSVILLE	(205)534-8524
MOBILE	(334)478-1679
MONTGOMERY	(334)281-2424
MUSCLE SHOALS	(205)767-3969
SELMA	(334)872-2074
SYLACAUGA	(205)249-3378
SYLVANIA	(205)638-7308
TUSCALOOSA	(205)759-2407

ALASKA		
ANCHORAGE	(907)272-2312
FAIRBANKS	(907)456-7501
HOMER	(907)235-6822
JUNEAU	(907)586-1161
KETCHIKAN	(907)225-5154
KODIAK	(907)486-2262
SITKA	(907)747-8886
SOLDOTNA	(907)262-5418
VALDEZ	(907)835-2726

ARIZONA		
BULLHEAD C.	(520)763-5105
CAMP VERDE	(520)567-6556
CASA GRANDE	(520)426-9318
COTTONWOOD	(520)634-0854
FLAGSTAFF	(520)779-3569
LK. HAVASU CITY	(520)453-1616
MESA	(602)834-9033
NOGALES	(520)287-2585
PAGE	(520)645-2711
PAYSON	(520)474-7104
PEORIA	(520)979-5843
PHOENIX	(602)264-1341
Span	(602)273-6352
PRESCOTT	(520)445-8691
RIVIERA	(520)763-4499
SEDONA	(520)282-5228
SHOW LOW	(520)537-7800
TUCSON	(520)624-4183
TDD	(520)882-7422
Span	(520)294-3282
WINSLOW	(520)289-3385
YUMA	(520)782-2605

ARKANSAS		
BATESVILLE	(501)793-3857
BEEBE	(501)882-3480
BISMARCK	(501)865-2353
BLYTHEVILLE	(501)763-2939
CAMDEN	(501)836-9946
CONWAY	(501)329-2151
DANVILLE	(501)495-7258
EL DORADO	(501)783-0123
FAYETTEVILLE	(800)738-2222
FORT SMITH	(501)783-0123

HEBER SPRINGS	(501)362-7026
HOT SPRINGS	(501)624-9214
KENNETT	(501)268-8509
LITTLE ROCK	(501)664-7303
MTN. HOME	(501)425-7234
NEWPORT	(501)523-8033
ROGERS	(501)636-2387
RUSSELLVILLE	(501)968-5046
SEARCY	(501)268-8509
W. MEMPHIS	(501)454-1441

CALIFORNIA		
ALAMEDA	(510)523-1843
ALTURAS	(916)233-2157
ANAHEIM	(714)535-0900
APPLE VALLEY	(619)242-9292
ARROYO GRANDE	(805)481-8619
AUBURN	(916)885-2235
AVALON	(310)510-2545
BAKERSFIELD	(805)322-4025
BARSTOW	(619)256-9766
BIG BEAR LAKE	(714)866-2765
BISHOP	(619)873-6700
BLYTHE	(619)922-3857
BURNEY	(916)335-2404
CALISTOGA	(707)963-6054
CAMARILLO	(805)389-1444
CAMBRIA	(805)927-0347
CATHEDRAL CITY	(619)324-4880
CHICO	(916)342-5756
CLAREMONT	(818)914-1861
	(714)626-2884
CLOVIS	(209)221-6907
COLTON	(909)825-4700
TDD	(909)825-3267
CRESCENT CITY	(707)464-3411
DAVIS	(916)756-2829
DUBLIN	(510)829-0666
EL CENTRO	(619)352-0807
EL CERRITO	(510)233-3110
EL MONTE	(818)350-9785
EL TORRO	(714)581-2694
EUREKA	(707)442-0711
FARMERSVILLE	(209)747-1277
FORT BRAGG	(707)964-7726
FRAZIER PARK	(805)245-1208
FREMONT	(510)791-9981
FRESNO	(209)221-6907
Span	(209)222-0496
FULLERTON	(714)773-4357
GILROY	(408)848-6928
GLENDALE	(818)957-9900
GLENDORA	(818)914-1861
HANFORD	(209)583-2521
HAWTHORNE	(213)675-2624
HERMOSA BEACH	(310)379-3413
HOLLISTER	(408)637-2156
HUNTINGTON PK.	(213)582-2439
INDIO Span	(619)347-2359
JACKSON	(209)223-4989
LA PUENTE	(818)333-4722
LAKE ISABELLA	(619)379-4112
LANCASTER	(805)945-5757
LAWNDALE	(310)644-1139
LIVINGSTON	(209)394-3937
LOMPOC	(805)737-1101

LONG BEACH	(562)493-5323
L. A. Central	(213)936-4343
Span	(213)384-2449
Hrng.Imp.	(213)387-7384
Span	(213)722-4175
E.OLYMPIC BL.	(213)725-9373
Span	(213)747-3273
Western	(310)474-7339
LOWER LAKE	(707)995-3316
MADERA	(209)674-1483
MAMMOTH LAKE	(619)934-3434
MANTECA	(209)825-7541
MARIN COUNTY	(415)499-0400
MARIPOSA	(209)966-3110
MISSION VIEJO	(714)581-2694
MODESTO	(209)572-4668
MONTCLAIR	(909)591-1249
MONTEREY	(408)373-3713
MT. SHASTA	(916)926-4353
NAPA	(707)255-4900
NEEDLES	(619)326-3434
NEWARK	(510)791-9692
NEWHALL	(805)259-0802
N. HLYWD. Span	(818)506-9360
N. HOLLYWOOD	(818)768-6975
OAKHURST	(209)683-7360
OAKLAND	(510)839-8900
Span	(510)261-2540
OXNARD	(805)486-7616
PALMS	(619)367-6121
PARADISE	(916)877-5456
PASO ROBLES	(805)238-3311
PETALUMA	(707)762-5122
PICO RIVERA	(310)699-9130
PLACERVILLE	(916)622-3500
PLEASNTN VLY	(510)829-0666
PLUMAS COUNTY	(916)283-9651
POMONA	(714)623-4415
PORTOLA	(916)832-5595
REDDING	(916)225-8955
RIDGECREST	(619)375-5445
SACRAMENTO	(916)454-1100
ST. HELENA	(707)963-2003
SALINAS	(408)424-9874
	(408)757-8518
SAN CLEMENTE	(408)757-8518
SAN DIEGO	(760)492-9226
	(760)265-8762
Span	(760)233-5899
SAN FRANCISCO	(415)621-1326
Span	(415)554-8811
TDD	(415)621-3481
SAN GABRIEL	(818)442-3933
SAN JOSE TDD	(415)621-1326
	(408)251-9292
Span	(408)259-6533
SAN L. OBISPO	(805)545-3211
SAN MATEO	(415)573-6811
SAN RAFAEL	(415)499-0400
SANTA ANA TDD	(714)556-4555
SANTA BARB'A	(805)962-3332
SANTA CLARA	(408)297-3555
Span	(408)258-7857
SANTA CRUZ	(408)457-2559
SANTA ROSA	(707)544-1300

INTERGROUP PHONE NUMBERS

SIMI VALLEY (805)522-9737
TDD (805)522-6221
SONOMA (707)938-2027
SOLVANG (805)688-4304
STOCKTON (209)464-1594
TDD/TTY (209)943-1744
SUSANVILLE (916)257-2880
TEHACHAPI (805)822-0643
TEMECULA (909)695-1535
TRACY (209)836-0803
TWAIN HARTE (209)533-1134
29 PALMS (619)367-6121
UPVALLEY (707)963-4673
VACAVILLE (707)446-2244
VALLEJO (707)643-8217
VAN NUYS (818)988-3001
Span (818)376-1417
Span (818)901-0976
TDD Only (818)988-0342
VISALIA (209)636-3432
VISTA (619)758-2514
WALNUT CR. (510)939-4155
WATSONVILLE (408)724-9855
Span (408)724-7270
WESTLAKE VIL. (805)495-1111
WOODLAND (916)662-3773

COLORADO
ARVADA (303)420-6560
ASPEN (970)928-0499
AURORA (303)695-7766
BAYFIELD (970)884-2338
BOULDER (303)447-8201
BRIGHTON (303)659-9953
CAMPO (719)787-2426
CANON CITY (719)584-9998
CO. SPRINGS TDD (719)634-5020
COMTRCE CITY (303)287-9950
CORTEZ (970)565-6242
CRAIG (970)824-7320
CRESTED BUTTE (303)349-7270
DENVER TDD (303)322-4440
DILLON (303)468-8100
DINOSAUR (970)374-2833
DOLORES (970)565-6333
DURANGO (970)247-1706
ESTES PARK (970)586-2711
FORT COLLINS (970)224-3552
FORT MORGAN (970)867-3461
GLENWD'SPR (970)945-5960
GRAND JUNCTION (970)245-9649
GREELEY (970)352-9852
HOLYOKE (970)854-3474
IGNACIO (970)563-4176
LA JUNTA (719)384-5791
LAKEWOOD (303)233-9703
LONGMONT (970)776-5714
LOVELAND (970)491-9324
MANCOS (970)533-7061
MARVEL (970)588-3304
MEEKER (970)878-4462
OAK CREEK (970)736-2640
PAGOSA SPRINGS (970)731-5496
PLAINS (970)848-5561
PUEBLO (719)584-9998
RANGELY (970)675-2542
SILVERTON (970)387-5388
STEAMBOAT SPR. (970)879-4882
STERLING (970)522-4538
TELLURIDE (800)367-7436
VAIL (970)476-0572
VALLECITO (970)563-4684
WRAY (970)332-4595

YUMA (970)848-5561

CONNECTICUT
BRIDGEPORT (203)333-5804
DANBURY (203)743-8959
DERBY (203)734-0312
GREENWICH (203)869-5221
GROTON (860)445-4443
HARTFORD (860)282-5924
LITCHFIELD (800)829-1863
MADISON (203)245-1212
MANCHESTER (860)646-2355
MIDDLETOWN (860)344-1744
NEW BRITAIN (860)223-9909
NEW HAVEN (203)624-6063
Span (203)773-3004
NEW LONDON (860)445-4443
NEW MILFORD (203)354-9843
NORWALK HELP (203)855-0075
SOUTHINGTON (860)621-2523
STAMFORD (203)323-3115
WALLINGFORD (203)265-5445
WATERBURY (203)755-2124
WESTPORT (203)227-2496

DELAWARE
DOVER (302)736-1567
GEORGETOWN (302)856-6452
WILMINGTON (302)655-5113

FLORIDA
BRADENTON (813)746-0999
BUSHNELL (352)793-7100
CLEARWATER (813)446-0938
COCOA (407)724-2247
COCOA BEACH (407)783-5831
CRESTVIEW (904)682-9832
DANIA (954)923-0311
DAYTONA BEACH (904)756-2930
DELAND (904)574-0204
DELRAY BEACH (561)276-4581
FLAGLER (904)445-4357
FT LAUDERDALE (954)584-8032
(305)462-0265
FT MYERS (813)275-5111
FT PIERCE (561)461-1799
FT WALTON BE (904)244-2421
GAINESVILLE (352)372-8091
HOLLYWOOD (954)875-2101
French (954)966-3773
ISLAMORADA (305)664-8683
JACKSONVILLE (904)399-8535
KEY LARGO (305)852-6186
KEY WEST (305)296-8654
KISS.-ST. CLOUD (407)957-8100
LAKELAND (813)687-9275
LARGO (813)530-0415
LEESBURG (352)360-0960
MARATHON (305)743-3262
MARCO ISLAND (941)394-6401
MELBOURNE (407)724-2247
MIAMI (305)887-6762
NAPLES (941)262-6535
NEW PT RICHEY (813)845-1652
NEW SMYRNA (904)423-6205
NORTHPORT (813)426-7723
NORTH BEAL (904)243-4590
OCALA (352)867-0660
OKEECHOBEE (Fr.) (561)763-1764
ORLANDO (407)617-3333
PALM CITY (286)286-7139
PALM COAST (904)445-4357
PANAMA CITY (904)784-7431
PENSACOLA (904)433-4191

PERRY (904)584-670
PINELLAS COUNTY (813)530-041
PINELLAS PARK (813)545-410
POMPANO BEACH (561)941-989
PORT ST. JOE (904)229-811
ST. AUGUSTINE (904)829-177
SAINT CLOUD (407)957-870
SARASOTA (813)951-683
SEBRING (813)382-266
S. PALM BEACH (561)276-498
SPRING HILL (352)683-459
STUART (561)283-933
TALLAHASSEE (904)385-155
TAMPA (813)933-912
TDD (813)933-972
TAVARES (904)343-261
TITUSVILLE (407)267-341
VENICE (813)408-979
VERO BEACH (561)562-111
WARM MIN. SPR. (813)625-196
W. PALM BEACH (561)844-880
WINTER HAVEN (813)294-144
ZEPHYRHILLS (901)567-059

GEORGIA
ALBANY (912)435-226
ALMA (912)632-686
AMERICUS (912)924-610
ATHENS (706)543-043
ATLANTA (404)525-313
AUGUSTA (706)860-833
BAINBRIDGE (912)246-257
BAXLEY (912)367-600
BLAKELY (912)723-549
BRUNSWICK (912)265-089
CAIRO (912)377-200
CAMILLA (912)336-847
COLUMBUS (706)327-607
CORDELE (912)273-904
DAWSONVILLE (706)265-700
DOUGLAS (912)384-865
DOUGLASVILLE (770)489-144
DUBLIN (912)272-677
FITZGERALD (912)423-563
GAINESVILLE (706)534-377
HARTWELL (706)376-885
JESUP (912)427-404
JONESBORO (706)228-435
LAWRENCEVL (770)474-261
MACON (912)746-665
METTER (912)685-255
MILLEDGEVLE (912)453-842
NO. GEORGIA (800)869-721
PERRY (912)987-566
ROME (706)295-975
SAINT MARYS (912)882-383
SANDERSVILLE (912)552-911
SAVANNAH (912)354-099
STATESBORO (912)764-421
SWAINSBORO (912)237-406
THOMASVILLE (912)226-106
TIFTON (912)386-160
VIDALIA (912)537-431
VIENNA (912)268-987
WARNER RBNS (912)923-765
WASHINGTON (706)678-498
WAYCROSS (912)285-118

HAWAII
HILO (808)961-613
HONOLULU (808)946-143
KAILUA KONA (808)329-121
KAUAI (808)245-667
MAUI (808)244-567

INTERGROUP PHONE NUMBERS

IDAHO
City	Number
)ISE	(208)344-6611
)ER D'ALENE	(208)667-4633
ETCHUM	(208)726-4650
OSCOW	(208)882-1597
CATELLO	(208)235-2444
ANDPOINT	(208)263-2740

ILLINOIS
City	Number
.TON	(618)465-1612
NTIOCH	(847)395-4440
RLINGTON HTS.	(773)640-1424
ARTLETT	(773)830-6091
LLEVILLE	(618)277-3492
LVIDERE	(815)544-3883
OOMINGTON	(309)828-7092
ARBONDALE	(618)549-4633
NTRALIA	(618)532-5007
AMPAIGN	(217)373-4200
HICAGO Span	(312)278-6251
TDD	(312)346-1475
RYSTAL LK.	(815)555-3311
KALB	(800)452-7990
ECATUR	(217)422-3766
ES PLAINES Span	(773)298-6251
XON	(800)756-8386
OWNERS GROVE	(708)852-8895
GIN	(708)742-7870
MHURST	(708)833-7897
REEPORT	(815)235-8988
ALESBURG	(309)343-1530
GHLAND PK	(847)432-9601
CKSONVILLE	(217)243-2862
ANKAKEE	(815)939-9506
EWANEE	(309)856-7601
A SALLE	(815)223-7374
BERTYVILLE	(847)362-1811
ACOMB	(847)837-5039
AYWOOD	(773)681-2739
DLINE	(309)764-1016
T VERNON	(618)242-0302
APERVILLE	(773)355-2622
TTAWA	(815)434-0165
LATINE	(847)358-9694
NA	(217)562-5884
ARIS	(217)465-8071
KIN	(309)353-9432
ORIA	(309)673-1456
ONTIAC	(815)842-3656
OCHELLE	(815)562-8744
CKFORD	(815)968-0333
SHVILLE	(217)322-4373
CHARLES	(630)377-6610
ARTA	(618)443-2012
RINGFIELD	(217)525-9423
YLORVILLE	(217)824-3028
ASHINGTON	(309)745-9046
AUKEGAN	(847)623-9660
HEATON	(773)653-6556

INDIANA
City	Number
DERSON	(317)644-3212
GOLA	(219)426-5721
OOMINGTON	(812)334-8191
	(800)589-8913
LUMBUS	(812)546-0507
NKIRK	(317)768-6608
KHART	(219)295-8188
ANSVILLE	(812)464-2219
RT WAYNE	(219)426-5721
EENSBURG	(812)372-6368
RON	(219)996-2220
DIANAPOLIS	(317)632-7864

City	Number
KNOX	(219)772-7771
LAFAYETTE	(219)742-1666
LA PORTE	(219)325-5551
MARION	(317)662-1668
MERRILLVILLE	(219)980-3455
MICHIGAN CTY.	(219)872-7200
MUNCIE	(317)747-1004
NEW CASTLE	(317)521-4112
PLYMOUTH	(219)936-6888
PORTAGE	(219)763-6431
RICHMOND	(317)973-4876
SEYMOUR	(812)523-3771
SOUTH BEND	(219)234-7007
TERRE HAUTE	(812)234-0827
VINCENNES	(812)882-2800

IOWA
City	Number
AMES	(515)232-8642
ATLANTIC	(712)243-3988
BEACON	(515)673-3763
BETTENDORF	(319)359-4152
BLOOMFIELD	(515)675-3414
BOONE	(515)437-2128
BURLINGTON	(319)753-5924
CARDO	(515)923-3294
CENTERVILLE	(515)856-6705
CHARLES CITY	(515)228-7453
CLINTON	(319)242-8136
DAVENPORT	(319)324-5232
DECORAH	(319)382-5189
DENISON	(712)263-5021
DES MOINES	(515)282-8550
DUBUQUE	(319)557-9196
FT. MADISON	(319)372-6837
IOWA CITY	(319)338-9111
MARSHALLTN	(515)753-6314
MUSCATINE	(319)263-4407
NASHUA	(515)435-2247
OELWEIN	(319)283-3484
OSSIAN	(319)532-9210
SIOUX CITY	(712)252-1333
SPIRIT LAKE	(712)336-0657
STORM LAKE	(712)732-1724
STORY CITY	(515)733-5121
TINGLEY	(515)772-4788
WASHINGTON	(319)653-3428
WATERLOO	(319)234-9434
WAUKON	(319)568-2276
WEST POINT	(319)837-6389

KANSAS
City	Number
ARKANSAS CITY	(316)442-5880
ATCHISON	(913)367-1217
BURLINGTON	(316)364-5479
CARBONDALE	(913)862-9233
CAWKER CITY	(913)781-4972
CHANUTE	(316)431-1064
COLBY	(913)462-8810
COUNCIL GR.	(913)499-6422
DODGE CITY	(316)225-3400
EL DORADO	(316)321-2956
EMPORIA	(316)342-1761
GARDNER	(913)884-8082
GLEN ELDER	(913)545-3544
GREAT BEND	(316)793-3962
HAYS	(913)625-9860
HUGOTON	(316)544-8633
HUTCHINSON	(316)662-9614
JOHNSON	(316)492-6680
KANSAS CITY	(913)788-5172
LEAVENWORTH	(913)682-0511
LIBERAL	(316)624-4214
LYNDON	(913)828-3331
MARIENTHAL	(316)375-2758

City	Number
OLATHE	(913)471-4606
OSAGE CITY	(913)665-7607
PHILLIPSBURG	(913)543-8968
SALINA	(913)823-3338
SHAWNEE MSN	(913)432-7911
STRONG CITY	(316)273-8569
TOPEKA	(913)354-3888
ULYSSES	(316)356-3003
WELLINGTON	(316)326-5890
WICHITA	(316)684-3661
WINFIELD	(316)221-0799
YATES CENTER	(316)625-3126

KENTUCKY
City	Number
ALBANY	(606)387-8706
ASHLAND	(606)324-9111
BOWLING GRN	(502)782-5267
CORBIN	(606)528-7188
COVINGTON	(606)491-7181
GEORGETOWN	(502)863-9086
HAZARD	(606)436-2776
HENDERSON	(502)826-5389
LA CENTER	(502)665-5432
LEXINGTON	(606)276-2917
LOUISVILLE	(502)582-1849
MADISONVILLE	(502)821-0266
MIDDLESBORO	(606)248-0867
MUNFORDVLE	(502)524-4882
OWENSBORO	(502)683-0371

LOUISIANA
City	Number
ABBEVILLE	(318)893-4424
ALEXANDRIA	(318)641-0904
BATON ROUGE	(504)924-0030
BOSSIER CITY	(318)747-0411
CULLEN	(318)994-3160
DE RIDDER	(318)463-2227
EUNICE	(318)457-5898
GONZALES	(504)644-0330
GRETNA	(504)393-9787
HOUMA	(504)892-5168
JENNINGS	(318)824-4513
LAFAYETTE	(318)234-7814
LK. CHARLES	(318)437-3022
LAROSE	(501)693-4641
LEESVILLE	(318)238-2838
MANDEVILLE	(504)626-8311
MANY	(318)256-3919
MONROE	(800)371-4017
NATCHITOCH'S	(318)357-1331
NEW IBERIA	(318)364-2522
NEW ORLEANS	(504)525-1178
NEW ROADS	(504)638-3215
OPELOUSAS	(318)942-8218
RUSTON	(318)251-1269
SHREVEPORT	(318)227-8170
SLIDELL	(504)649-3206
SULPHUR	(318)527-0967
W. MONROE	(318)323-0070

MAINE
City	Number
AUGUSTA	(207)626-3727
BANGOR	(207)941-8326
BATH	(207)443-1336
BELFAST	(207)338-1496
BIDDEFORD	(207)282-7301
CAMDEN	(207)236-2013
DAMAR'SCO'TA	(207)882-9700
ELLSWORTH	(207)288-5915
FARMINGTON	(207)364-7911
FORT KENT	(207)739-7515
LEWISTON	(207)795-5844
MACHIAS	(207)369-7911
PORTLAND	(207)774-4335
PRESQUE ISLE	(207)764-8089

INTERGROUP PHONE NUMBERS

NEW MEXICO

City	Number
ALAMOGORDO	(505)437-5220
ALBUQUERQUE	(505)266-1900
CAPITAN	(505)354-2385
CLOVIS	(505)769-2718
DEMING	(505)546-4066
FARMINGTON	(505)327-0731
LAS CRUCES	(505)523-3128
LAS VEGAS	(505)425-3577
ROSWELL	(505)623-0166
RUIDOSO	(505)258-3643
SANTA FE	(505)982-8932
TAOS	(505)758-3318

NEW YORK

City	Number
ALBANY	(518)489-6779
BATAVIA	(716)548-7712
BELLEROSE	(718)520-5021
BINGHAMTON	(607)722-5983
BRONX	(718)515-8481
BROOKLYN	(718)339-4777
BUFFALO	(716)853-0388
CANTON	(315)268-0120
CATSKILL	(518)943-9394
CORNING	(607)737-6701
CORNWALL	(914)534-8525
ELMIRA	(607)734-8204
FREEPORT	(516)223-9590
GENESEE COUNTY	(716)548-7712
GENEVA	(315)789-9955
HUDSON	(800)872-7675
ITHACA	(607)273-1541
KINGSTON	(914)331-6360
LIBERTY	(914)295-1010
MT. VERNON	(914)664-8955
NEW YORK	(212)647-1680
	(212)683-9460
Span	(212)964-2560
NIAGARA FALLS	(716)285-5319
ONEONTA	(888)227-6237
PAINTED POST	(607)936-4295
PATCHOGUE	(516)669-1124
PLATTSBURGH	(518)561-8444
POUGHKEEPSIE	(914)452-1111
ROCHESTER	(716)232-6720
ROCKLAND CO.	(914)352-1112
S. GLENS FALLS	(518)793-1113
SPRING VALLEY	(914)352-1112
SYRACUSE	(315)463-5011
UTICA	(315)732-6880
WATERTOWN	(315)788-2280
WAVERLY	(717)888-7727
W. HEMPSTEAD	(516)292-3040
WHITE PLAINS	(914)949-1200

NORTH CAROLINA

City	Number
ABERDEEN	(919)695-1976
ASHEBORO	(919)629-7167
ASHEVILLE	(704)254-8539
BOONE	(704)264-1212
BURLINGTON	(919)228-7611
BUXTON	(919)995-4240
CHARLOTTE	(704)332-4387
DURHAM	(919)286-9499
ELIZABETH CITY	(919)338-1849
FAYETTEVILLE	(910)678-8002
GASTONIA	(704)865-5161
GREENSBORO	(919)854-4278
GREENVILLE	(919)758-0787
GARNER	(919)892-6089
HAVELOCK	(919)447-4245
JACKSONVILLE	(918)455-3666
JEFFERSON	(919)982-2641
KINSTON	(919)934-0490
LEXINGTON	(919)542-5198
RALEIGH	(919)783-6144
REIDSVILLE	(919)634-0905
ROANOKE RDS	(919)537-2242
SAMPSON	(919)592-2019
SANFORD	(919)776-5522
SHELBY	(704)484-1000
SMITHFIELD	(919)934-0490
STATESVILLE	(704)878-6444
WADESBORO	(704)694-6431
WASHINGTON	(919)975-6113
WAXHAW	(704)843-2847
WILKESBORO	(919)667-5833
WILMINGTON	(919)762-1230
WINSTON SALEM	(919)725-6031

NORTH DAKOTA

City	Number
BEULAH	(701)873-2284
DEVILS LAKE	(701)662-5876
EPPING	(701)859-3832
FARGO	(701)232-9930
GRAND FORKS	(701)772-7005
HAZEN	(701)748-2311
JAMESTOWN	(701)252-9493
LANGDON	(701)256-2256
PLAZA	(701)497-3818
STANLEY	(701)628-2952
TUTTLE	(701)867-2795
WILLISTON	(701)572-9882
WAHPETON	(218)643-2143

OHIO

City	Number
AKRON TDD	(330)253-8181
BELLEFONTINE	(513)599-4328
BOWLING GREEN	(419)352-1545
CANTON	(330)497-4427
CINCINNATI TDD	(513)861-9966
CLEVELAND	(440)241-7387
COLUMBUS	(614)253-8501
TTY-Hmg. Imp.	(614)253-5554
DAYTON TDD	(513)222-2211
FINDLAY	(419)423-6273
FREMONT	(419)625-5995
HAMILTON	(513)868-6127
HEATH TDD	(614)522-4513
JACKSON	(614)286-6790
LANCASTER	(614)653-4869
LIMA	(419)229-7484
LORAIN	(440)246-1800
MANSFIELD	(419)526-9524
MARIETTA	(614)373-3068
MARION	(614)382-1919
MIDDLETOWN	(513)423-0102
NEWARK	(614)345-7060
PORT CLINTON	(419)797-4135
SALEM	(330)337-1039
SANDUSKY	(419)625-5995
TOLEDO	(419)472-8242
TDD	(419)472-5162
WARREN	(330)652-9998
YOUNGSTOWN	(330)783-5000
ZANESVILLE	(614)452-2333

OKLAHOMA

City	Number
ALVA	(405)327-9923
BARTLESVILLE	(918)336-7904
CLAREMORE	(918)341-6418
DUNCAN	(405)255-3480
EDMOND	(405)340-7003
EL RENO	(405)262-1013
ELK CITY	(405)225-0851
ENID	(405)234-0400
FAIRVIEW	(405)227-9917
GUYMON	(405)338-6628
MADILL	(405)795-7771
MCALESTER	(918)423-0715
MUSKOGEE	(918)687-9426
OK. CITY TDD	(405)524-1100
Northside	(405)751-3888
OKMULGEE	(918)756-3638
PONCA CITY	(405)765-8462
SAPULPA	(918)224-9859
SHAWNEE	(405)273-9504
STILLWATER	(405)377-5803
TULSA	(918)627-2224

OREGON

City	Number
ALBANY	(541)967-6243
ASTORIA	(503)325-3580
BEND	(541)389-5724
BROOKINGS	(541)469-2440
BURNS	(541)573-7160
CAVE JNCTION	(541)592-4129
COOS BAY	(541)269-9331
CORVALLIS	(541)967-6243
DEPOE BAY	(541)765-3111
EUGENE	(541)342-4113
Span	(541)344-9728
GEARHART	(541)325-3580
GRANTS PASS	(541)474-0782
HEPPNER	(541)976-5531
HERMISTON	(541)567-2522
HOOD RIVER	(541)386-4116
KLAMATH FLS	(541)883-4970
LA GRANDE	(541)963-3758
LINCOLN CITY	(541)765-3111
MCMINNVILLE	(503)472-1172
MEDFORD	(541)773-4848
MOLALLA	(541)829-9090
NEWPORT	(541)265-8302
ONTARIO	(800)627-9103
PENDLETON	(541)276-3428
PORTLAND	(503)223-8569
ROSEBURG	(541)673-7552
SALEM	(503)399-0599
SEASIDE	(541)738-8310
SILETZ	(541)265-8302
SOUTHBEACH	(541)867-4848
STAYTON	(541)769-5468
THE DALLES	(541)296-1672
TILLAMOOK	(503)842-8958

PENNSYLVANIA

City	Number
ALLENTOWN	(610)434-0614
ALTOONA	(814)946-9069
ARDMORE	(215)642-9679
BEDFORD	(814)623-5996
BETHLEHEM	(610)882-0558
BRISTOL	(215)574-6900
BUTLER	(412)287-1815
CARLISLE	(717)249-6773
CHARLEROI	(412)489-0740
CHESTER	(215)497-9951
CLEARFIELD	(814)765-5341
DOYLESTOWN	(215)348-3393
DU BOIS	(814)371-0180
ERIE	(814)342-0162
GLENOLDEN	(215)532-9965
HARRISBURG	(717)234-5390
HAZLETON	(717)454-3173
HONESDALE	(717)253-5658
INDIANA	(412)349-4061
JACKSON CENTER	(412)342-0162
JOHNSTOWN	(814)533-5907
LANCASTER	(717)394-3238
LANSDALE	(215)723-7090
LEBANON	(717)274-1649
LEHIGHTON	(717)377-4303
LEVITTOWN	(215)788-0659

Location	Number
LEWISTOWN	(717)242-1517
MALVERN	(215)644-9675
MEADVILLE	(814)425-2675
MILFORD	(717)296-5344
OIL CITY	(800)227-2421
PHILADELPHIA	(215)574-6900
TDD	(215)574-6906
Span	(215)229-7540
PHOENIXVILLE	(215)933-9674
PITTSBURGH	(412)471-7472
PITTSTON	(717)564-0488
PITTSTON	(717)883-7261
POTTSTOWN	(215)323-3450
POTTSVILLE	(717)628-4550
READING	(610)373-6500
SCRANTON	(717)654-0488
SHARON	(412)342-0162
ST.COLLEGE	(814)237-3757
STROUDSBURG	(717)424-8532
SUNBURY	(717)286-7436
TARENTUM	(412)226-3203
TUNKHANOCK	(717)836-1234
UPPER DARBY	(215)352-9897
WARREN	(814)726-2345
WASHINGTON	(412)225-5820
WILKES BARRE	(717)829-0007
WILLIAMSPORT	(717)322-1022
WYOMING	(717)693-3594
YORK	(717)854-4617

RHODE ISLAND

Location	Number
NEWPORT	(401)846-2622
PROVIDENCE	
Cent. Office	(401)438-8860
TDD In State	(800)439-8860
Span	(401)946-0060
WARWICK	(401)739-8777
WOONSOCKET	(401)765-2525

SOUTH CAROLINA

Location	Number
AIKEN	(803)648-1509
BEAUFORT	(803)525-1834
CAMDEN	(803)432-9511
CHARLESTON	(803)554-2998
CHESTER	(803)385-6768
COLUMBIA	(803)254-5301
CONWAY	(803)248-4796
GREENVILLE	(864)233-6454
HILTON HEAD IS.	(803)842-6630
JEFFERSON	(803)658-7541
LANCASTER	(803)285-4131
LIBERTY	(864)843-2378
MONETTA	(803)285-5488
MYRTLE BCH	(803)293-7373
N. AUGUSTA	(803)279-1060
N.MYRTLE BEACH	(803)280-1476
ORANGEBURG	(803)534-4854
ST. MATTHEWS	(803)874-1547
SUMTER	(803)775-1852

SOUTH DAKOTA

Location	Number
ABERDEEN	(605)225-1292
BISON	(605)244-5575
BRANDON	(605)582-3833
FAULKTON	(605)598-4290
MILLER	(605)853-2421
MITCHELL	(605)342-9808
RAPID CITY	(605)394-9214
REDFIELD	(605)472-9993
SALEM	(605)247-3334
SIOUX FALLS	(605)338-6800
WATERTOWN	(605)886-9070
WINNER	(605)842-0312

TENNESSEE

Location	Number
BRISTOL	(423)968-2020
CHAPEL HILL	(615)364-7854
CHATTA'NOGA	(423)267-6277
CLARKSVILLE	(615)647-0225
CLEVELAND	(423)476-2969
COLUMBIA	(615)381-1048
CROSSVILLE	(615)484-6477
DICKSON	(615)952-6185
GATLINBURG	(423)522-9667
JACKSON	(901)989-3668
JOHNSON CITY	(423)928-0871
KINGSPORT	(423)245-1440
KNOXVILLE	(423)522-9667
LEWISBURG	(615)359-5927
LYNCHBURG	(615)759-7274
LINDEN	(615)589-3344
MANCHESTER	(615)728-6285
MARYVILLE	(423)983-8300
MEMPHIS	(901)454-1414
MORRISTOWN	(615)586-9866
MURFREESBORO	(615)893-0854
NASHVILLE	(615)831-1050
OAK RIDGE	(423)482-5200
PULASKI	(615)363-1854
SHELBYVILLE	(615)684-5591
TULLAHOMA	(615)455-4843
WINCHESTER	(615)962-4545

TEXAS

Location	Number
ABILENE	(915)673-2711
ALICE	(512)668-2525
ALPINE	(915)837-5578
ALVIN	(713)585-9669
AMARILLO	(806)374-8484
ANDREWS	(915)523-2364
ANGLETON	(409)849-8080
ARLINGTON	(817)261-8616
AUSTIN	(512)494-0760
Span	(512)441-3369
BALLINGER	(915)657-6645
BASTROP	(512)321-2443
BAYTOWN	(713)427-2500
BEAUMONT	(409)835-6347
BEDFORD	(817)283-1250
BELLAIRE	(713)668-9952
BIG SPRING	(915)267-9144
BORGER	(806)273-5001
BROWNSVILLE	(512)544-8530
Span	(512)542-7874
BROWNWOOD	(915)646-4144
BRYAN	(409)361-7976
CLEBURNE	(817)645-9959
CLUTE	(409)265-8066
COLUMBUS	(409)732-3079
CONROE	(409)756-9447
CORPUS CHR'TI	(512)852-0234
CORSICANA	(214)874-6121
DALLAS TDD	(214)823-3200
Span	(214)827-9227
DEL RIO	(512)775-7008
	(512)774-2641
DENISON	(903)465-4430
DENTON	(817)566-9110
DUNCANVILLE	(214)709-8553
EAGLE LAKE	(409)234-3933
EL CAMPO	(409)453-0071
EL PASO	(915)562-4081
Span	(915)778-2334
FARMERS BRANCH	(214)875-1550
FORT DAVIS	(915)426-3145
FT. STOCKTON	(915)336-6546
FORT WORTH	(817)332-3533
Hearing-Impair.	(817)293-1434
GALVESTON	(409)763-9276
GATESVILLE	(817)865-93..
GEORGETOWN	(512)863-85..
GILMER	(903)734-54..
GRAND PRAIRIE	(214)660-52..
GRAPEVINE	(817)488-96..
GREENVILLE	(903)455-86..
HARLINGEN	(210)428-95..
HASKELL	(817)864-27..
HEMPHILL	(409)787-26..
HEMPSTEAD	(409)826-65..
HOUSTON	(713)686-63..
TTY	(713)520-63..
Eve/Wknds (Voice/TTY)	(713)864-34..
Span	(713)864-74..
HUMBLE	(713)358-59..
HUNTSVILLE	(409)291-33..
HURST	(817)282-96..
INGLESIDE	(512)776-34..
IRAAN	(915)639-28..
IRVING	(214)579-96..
JACKSONVILLE	(903)586-07..
JASPER	(409)384-61..
KATY	(713)686-63..
KERMIT	(915)586-68..
KERRVILLE	(512)257-67..
KILGORE	(903)984-08..
KINGSVILLE	(512)592-57..
LAMESA	(806)872-37..
LAREDO	(512)721-1..
LEWISVILLE	(214)420-0..
LIVINGSTON	(409)967-0..
LONGVIEW	(903)753-60..
LUBBOCK	(806)763-11..
MANSFIELD	(817)473-66..
MARFA	(915)729-44..
McKINNEY	(214)548-9..
McALLEN	(210)686-8..
MERCEDES	(210)428-9..
MESQUITE	(214)279-96..
MIDLAND	(915)684-94..
MT. PLEASANT	(903)572-22..
NEDERLAND	(409)724-6..
NEW BRAUNF'L	(512)620-44..
NEWTON	(409)379-8..
ODESSA	(915)337-96..
ORANGE	(409)886-9..
ORE CITY	(903)968-3..
PALESTINE	(903)729-1..
PAMPA	(806)665-69..
PARIS	(903)785-55..
PERRYTON	(806)435-2..
PLANO East	(214)424-9..
PLANO West	(214)867-1..
PORT ARANSAS	(512)749-64..
PORT ARTHUR	(409)985-95..
PORT NECHES	(409)722-5..
PROSPER	(214)347-2..
RICHARDSON	(214)690-5..
ROCKPORT	(512)729-7..
ROUND ROCK	(512)255-..
SAN ANGELO	(915)657-6..
SAN ANTONIO	(210)828-6..
Span	(210)225-..
SAN BENITO	(210)428-9..
SAN MARCOS	(512)396-34..
SANFORD	(806)373-..
SANTA FE	(409)925-..
SEABROOK	(713)474-55..
SEGUIN	(512)379-..
SHERMAN	(903)868-..
SILSBEE	(409)385-..

INTERGROUP PHONE NUMBERS

SINTON	(512)364-1158
SULPHUR SPRINGS	(903)885-0295
SWEETWATER	(915)236-6918
TAFT	(512)528-3142
TARPLEY	(512)562-3243
TEMPLE	(817)770-4629
TERRELL	(214)563-2705
TEXARKANA	(903)772-1463
TEXAS CITY	(409)942-4417
THE WOODLANDS	(713)363-4854
TOMBALL	(713)255-3022
UVALDE	(512)278-9478
VERNON	(817)552-6833
VICTORIA	(512)575-0200
WACO	(817)754-3336
WAXAHACHIE	(214)937-5261
WEATHERFRD	(817)598-9021
WESLACO	(612)968-5228
WHARTON	(409)532-1062
WICHITA FLS	(817)322-3213

UTAH

BRIGHAM CITY	(801)723-1177
CASTLE DALE	(801)381-2400
FERRON	(801)384-2574
LOGAN	(801)752-2333
MOAB	(801)259-7556
OGDEN	(801)393-4728
ORANGEVILLE	(801)748-2233
OREM	(801)375-8620
PARK CITY	(801)649-0022
PRICE	(801)637-7629
PROVO	(801)375-8620
SALT L'KE CITY	(801)484-7871
ST.GEORGE	(801)673-3936
VERNAL	(801)789-0914

VERMONT

ARLINGTON	(802)375-9292
BENNINGTON	(802)447-1285
BRATTLEBORO	(802)257-0665
BURLINGTON	(802)658-4221
DORSET	(802)362-3824
MANCHESTER	(802)362-2545
MIDDLEBURY	(802)388-9284
RUTLAND	(802)775-0402
ST.ALBANS	(802)524-5444
S.JOHNSBURY	(802)748-3708
WATERBURY	(802)229-5100
WHITE RIVER	(802)295-7611

VIRGINIA

ALEXANDRIA	(703)739-0058
ARLINGTON	(703)486-2291
AVON	(540)456-8531
BIG STONE GAP	(703)523-4545
BOONES MILL	(540)334-2055
BUENA VISTA	(540)463-3411
CHARLOTTSV'LE	(804)293-6565
COVINGTON	(540)962-1037
DANVILLE	(540)792-4013
FALLS CHURCH	(703)549-3956
FORT LEE	(804)732-7361
FREDERICKSBG.	(540)373-2028
GLOUCESTER	(757)693-5838
HAMPTON	(898)898-5829
HARBORTON	(757)442-3456
HARRISONBURG	(703)434-8870
HEATHSVILLE	(757)580-5209
KILMARNOCK	(757)435-1081
LEXINGTON	(540)463-3411
LYNCHBURG	(540)847-4733
MARTINSVILLE	(540)632-5111
MATHEWS	(757)725-7176
NEWPORT NEWS	(757)877-0600
RICHMOND	(804)355-1212
ROANOKE	(540)343-6857
STAFFORD	(703)659-4248
STAUNTON	(703)885-6912
TAPPAHAN'CK	(540)443-3769
VIENNA	(703)281-7015
VIRGINIA B'CH	(757)490-3980
WARSAW	(757)333-4851
WAYNESBORO	(703)949-7777
WILLIAMSBURG	(757)220-4303
WINCHSTR TDD	(703)667-0322
WOODLAWN	(540)236-6503

WASHINGTON

ABERDEEN	(206)532-2691
BELLEVUE	(425)454-9192
BELLINGHAM	(206)734-1688
BREMERTON	(800)562-7455
CENTRALIA	(360)330-1416
CLARKSTON	(509)758-2821
CLE ELUM	(509)649-3133
COLVILLE	(509)684-3000
EDMONDS	(425)672-0987
ELLENSBURG	(509)925-2494
EVERETT	(425)252-2525
FRIDAY HARBOR	(206)378-3521
GIG HARBOR	(253)858-3144
KENNEWICK	(509)735-4086
KITSAP CNTY	(800)562-7455
LONGVIEW	(206)423-2250
NORTH BEACH	(206)642-2902
OAK HARBOR	(206)675-3843
OKANOGAN	(509)826-6299
OLYMPIA	(206)352-7344
PT. ORCHARD	(206)876-6642
PT. TOWNSEND	(206)385-6026
PULLMAN	(208)882-1597
PUYALLUP	(253)841-4158
ROSLYN	(509)649-3133
SEATTLE TDD	(206)587-2838
SEDRO WOOLLEY	(206)826-4226
SPANAWAY	(206)474-8897
SPOKANE	(509)624-1442
SUNNYSIDE	(509)837-5801
TACOMA TDD	(253)474-8897
TOPPENISH	(509)865-5757
VANCOUVER	(206)694-3870
VASHON	(206)463-5556
WALLA WALLA	(509)525-1122
WENATCHEE	(509)663-5104
WESTPORT	(206)268-0607
YAKIMA	(509)453-7680

WASHINGTON, D.C.

WASHINGTON	(202)966-9115
Span	(202)797-9738
TDD/Voice	(202)966-9782

WEST VIRGINIA

STATEWIDE	(800)333-5051

WISCONSIN

APPLETON	(414)731-4331
ASHLAND	(715)682-4460
BALDWIN	(715)684-2799
CRIVITZ	(715)854-2410
BARRONNETT	(715)822-4805
BLOOMER	(715)568-4164
EAU CLAIRE	(715)832-3234
FOND DU LAC	(414)922-7512
GREEN BAY	(414)494-9904
JANESVILLE	(608)754-1766
JEFFERSON CO.	(414)699-5967
KENOSHA	(414)654-8246
LA CROSSE	(608)782-1045
MADISON	(608)222-8989
MAYVILLE	(414)387-5710
MEDFORD	(715)748-3230
MENOMONIE	(715)235-9145
MILWAUKEE	(414)771-9119
OCONTO FLS.	(414)846-8144
OSHKOSH	(414)236-6322
RACINE	(414)886-7788
SISTER BAY	(414)854-5953
STOUGHTON	(608)873-6004
STURGEON BAY	(414)743-0900
SUPERIOR	(715)394-9824
WAUSAU	(715)842-1120
WEST BEND	(414)338-1101

WYOMING

BAGGS	(307)383-2480
BUFFALO	(307)684-9414
CASPER	(307)234-1447
CHEYENNE	(307)632-7706
CODY	(307)587-3024
EVANSTON	(307)789-9119
GILLETTE	(307)686-6107
KEMMERER	(307)877-6600
LARAMIE	(307)745-3322
LUSK	(307)334-3739
NEWCASTLE	(307)746-4457
ROCK SPRINGS	(307)362-8421
SHERIDAN	(307)672-6257

OUTSIDE U.S.A. - TELEPHONE LIST
ENGLISH SPEAKING

AUSTRALIA

ADELAIDE	08-346-4044
ALICE SPRINGS	089-524404
BALLINA	066-86-8599
BRISBANE	07-210-0162
CAIRNS	077-51-2872
CANBERRA	062-491-340
DARWIN	089-819216
EAST PERTH	09-325-3209
GEELONG	052-91-710
GOSFORD	043-233890
HAMILTON	049-692196
HOBART	02-34-8711
LAUNCESTON	003-31-3355
LITHGOW	063-53-1241
MANILLA	067-851314
MELBOURNE	03-429-1833
NEWCASTLE	049-246-111
PERTH	61-9-3253946
SOUTHPORT	075-912062
ST.IVES	02-488-9820
SYDNEY(GSO)	61-2-663-1206
SYDNEY	61-2-799-1199
TOOWAMBA	076-322466
TOWNSVILLE	077-756755
WOLLONGONG	042-295-241

BAHAMAS

NASSAU	242322-1685

BAHRAIN

MANAMA	687-538

BARBADOS

ST. MICHAEL	2464369593

INTERGROUP PHONE NUMBERS

BERMUDA
HAMILTON	441 236 8293

CANADA
BARRIE	(705) 728-6581
CALGARY	(403) 777-1212
CAMPBELL R.	(250) 287-4343
CANNING	(902) 582-7007
CHETWYND	(250) 788-3629
CORNWALL	(613) 938-1984
COURTENAY	(250) 334-8042
DARTMOUTH	(902) 461-1119
DRUMNDV'LLE	(819) 478-7030
DUNCAN	(250) 746-4913
EDMONTON	(403) 424-5900
ELLIOT LAKE	(705) 461-3150
FT. MCMURR'Y	(403) 743-0099
FT. NELSON	(250) 774-7711
FT. SAINT JOHN	(250) 785-8866
FRASER VLY.	(604) 792-1461
GANDER	(709) 651-2001
GRAND FALLS	(709) 489-5443
GULF ISLANDS	(250) 537-2135
HAMILTON	(905) 522-8392
LETHBRIDGE	(403) 327-8049
KAMLOOPS	(250) 374-2456
KELOWNA	(250) 860-1828
KITCHENER	(519) 742-6183
LAVAL	(514) 682-2470
LAVAL	(514) 682-2470
LONDON	(519) 438-9006
MEDICINE HAT	(403) 527-8601
MONTREAL	(514) 731-4188
Span	(514) 670-9480
Sud - Ouest	(514) 374-5868
Central	(514) 376-9230
NANAIMO	(604) 753-7513
OSHAWA	(905) 728-1020
OTTAWA	(613) 237-6000
PEMBROKE	(613) 732-7831
PENTICTON	(604) 493-1474
PETERBOR'GH	(705) 745-6111
PRIN. GEORGE	(250) 564-7550
QUEBEC	(418) 529-0015
QUEBEC	(418) 877-9568
REGINA	(306) 545-9340
ST. JOHN'S	(709) 579-5215
ST. CATHERIN'S	(905) 935-9833
ST. THOMAS	(519) 633-0430
SALMON ARM	(250) 832-6019
SASKATOON	(306) 665-6727
SLT STE. MAR'I	(705) 254-1312
SUDBURY	(705) 674-6217
SWIFT CUR'NT	(306) 773-7494
THUNDER BAY	(807) 344-1712
TIMMINS	(705) 264-9964
TORONTO TDD	(416) 487-5591
Span	(416) 667-0238
VANCOUVER	(604) 434-3933
TDD	(604) 434-2553
VERNON	(250) 545-4933
VICTORIA	(250) 383-3260
WINNIPEG	(204) 942-0126
WINDSOR	(519) 326-3234
WOODSTOCK	(519) 537-2894
WHITEHORSE	(403) 668-2827

CHANNEL ISLANDS
GUERNSEY	0481-713480
JERSEY	0534-26681

ENGLAND
BARNSTABLE	01271-79695
BEDFORD	01234-360011
BIRMINGHAM	01121-212911
BLACKPOOL	01253-792632
BOURNEMOUTH	01202-296600
BRIGHTON	01273-203343
BRISTOL	0117-926-5520
CAMBORNE	01209-719200
CAMBRIDGE	01223-883906
CORNWALL	01209-719200
COVENTRY	01203-612211
DERBYSHIRE	0115-941700
DEVON	01392-221444
DORSET	01202-296600
ESSEX	01245-256147
EXETER	01392-437497
GLOUCESTER	01452-418515
GR YARMOUTH	01493-440396
HARLOW	01279-454502
HEREFORD	01432-356336
HERTFORDSHR	01234-360011
HIGH WYCOMBE	01494-449691
HUMBERSIDE	01482-830083
IPSWICH	01473-212224
ISLE OF MAN	01624-663676
KENT-EAST	01227-455557
KENT-WEST	01622-751842
KINGS LYNN	01553-772373
LEICESTERSHIRE	0116-29417100
LIVERPOOL	01151-7092900
LONDON	01171-3523001
MANCHESTER	0161-236-6556
MID SURREY	01252-521133
NEWCASTLE	0191-261-877
NORTHAMPTON	01604-37788
NORTHDOWN	01962-878866
NORWICH	01603-621128
NOTTINGHAM	01602-417100
OLDHAM	0161-633-1122
OXFORD	01865-242373
PLYMOUTH	01752-791111
PORTSMOUTH	01705-580776
READING	01734-597494
REDDITCH	01527-64715
SCARBOROUGH	01723-35368
SHEFFIELD	01114-2701984
SOUTHAMPTON	01703-223198
S. BEDF'RDSHIRE	01582-484948
S. HUMBERSIDE	01472-362058
STEVENAGE	01438-747475
STOKE ON TR'NT	01782-266366
SUSSEX	01622-751842
TORQUAY	01803-298000
WILTSHIRE	01380-720064
WOLVERHMPT'N	01902-758555
WOODSTOCK	01993-813351
YORKSHIRE	01532-454567

FRANCE
PARIS	46-34-39-65

GERMANY
BERLIN	30-7875188
FRANKFURT	069-59-74-274
LAHR	7821-37977
MANNHEIM	621-291441
MUNICH	0911-755951

GREENLAND
NUUK	(299) 24858

GUAM
TUMO	(671) 646-1006

HONG KONG
HONG KONG	522-5665

IRELAND
DUBLIN	0001-538998
BELFAST	0232-681084
CORK	021-500481
LIMERICK	061-311222

ITALY
ROME	678-0320

JAMAICA
KINGSTON	809-926-5556

JAPAN
OKINAWA	634 HELP
KYOTO	0753 71 5649
TOKYO	(03)3971-147

KENYA
NAIROBI	254-2-56609

KOREA
SEOUL	027975861

MARSHALL ISLANDS
KWAJALEIN	(805) 238-79..

MEXICO
COZUMEL	21007
MEXICO CITY	511-1213

NETHERLANDS
AMSTERDAM	021-49481

NEW ZEALAND
AUCKLAND (GSO)	4-859455
AUCKLAND	093-666688
CHRISTCHURCH	03790860
WELLINGTON	4-4993681

PAPUA NEW GUINEA
PORT MORESBY	213401

PHILIPPINES
MANILA	63-2-1525001

PUERTO RICO
BAYAMON	(787) 786-828

SCOTLAND
NATIONWIDE	0345-697-55
ABERDEEN	0224-582184
ANGUS	01674-67880
ARGYLL	01631-56282
AYRSHIRE	0294-220069
DUMBARTON	01389-71060
DUNDEE	01382-22352
EDINBURGH	031-225-272
ELGIN	0343-45870
GLASGOW	041-221-902
PERTH	01738-63999

SINGAPORE
SINGAPORE	65-338-2791

SOUTH AFRICA
BENONI	11-4211534
CAPE TOWN	021-24-7559
DURBAN	031-301-495
EAST RAND	011-421-153
JOHANNES'B'RG	011-640-714
JOHANNES'B'RG	011-483-247
JOHANNES'B'RG	011-483-247
PIETRMARITZB'RG	0331-45-679
PORT ELIZABETH	041-55-4019
PRETORIA	012-322-604
VAAL TRIANGLE	016-33-534

SOUTH PACIFIC
NORFOLK ISLAND	2899

SPAIN
MADRID	13091947

SRI LANKA
COLOMBO	1-582814

ST. MARTIN
PHILIPSBURG	5995-25742

SWEDEN
BENIDORM	5730605

THAILAND
BANGKOK	256-6422

TRINIDAD AND TOBAGO
NTROSE 809-664-5854
TURKEY
KARA 433-4607
VIRGIN ISLANDS, U.S.
HOMAS (809)776-5283

WALES
ABERYSTWYTH 01970 625574
CARDIFF 01222-373939
CARMARTHEN 01267 238888
GWYNEDD 01248-716947

NEATH 01639644871
PEMBROKE 01646-695555
TELFORD 01952 270616
ZIMBABWE
BULAWAYO 74111

NON ENGLISH-SPEAKING

ARGENTINA
ENOS AIRES 855-1813
LLANEDA 201-7943
US ESTE 241-6774
CUARTO 0586-22957
ISIDRO 743-9584
AUSTRIA
NNA 222-78-82-41
BELARUS
SK 71 72-603911
BELGIUM
SSELS 322-5132336
AING 32-(0) 41-372620
BOLIVIA
NTA CRUZ LA SIERRA 591 33-325180
BRAZIL
ACAJU 079-211-2027
EM 091-224-2965
O HORIZONTE 031-224-774
ASILIA 061-226-0091
CHOEIRO ITAPEM 027-522-0648
MPO GRANDE 067-383-1854
ABA 065-321-1020
RITIBA 041-222-2422
QUE DE CAXIAS 4-0104
RIANOPOLIS 0482-22-6713
TALEZA 085-231-2437
ANIA 062-223-0445
EUS 231-7418
INGA 031-821-3758
JAI 0473-4713
O PESSOA 083-222-2256
ZEIRO 085-511-2466
Z DE FORA 032-215-8503
CAPA 096-222-5154
CEIO 082-221-2611
NAUS 092-232-1717
TAL 084-221-3181
EROI 718-4956
OTAS 0532-25-0373
RTO ALEGRE 0512-24-0140
IFE 081-221-3592
ERGRUPO EGIDE 232-17-19
O LUIS 098-222-4050
REZINA 086-223-5919
AITABA 073-230-1442
ORIA 027-223-7268
CHILE
TIAGO 562-3211938
JPO ALTO APOLO 384782
PARAISO 230256
COLOMBIA
DELLIN 4-5124390
RRANQUILLA 310-317
OTA 2-84-34-28
CARAMANGA 424423
I 80-30-29

CARTAGENA 641-619
CARTAGO 29200
CUCUTA 718-726
MANIZALES 82-39-12
MEDELLIN 231-71-06
NEIVA 88-711480
POPAYAN 28-210165
VILLAVICENCIO 86-623030
COSTA RICA
SAN JOSE 222-5224
ALAJUELA 441-5891
DESAMPARADOS 259-6959
GOLFITO 253-9684
LIBERIA 666-2195
CYPRUS
NICOSIA 35-72-443751
DENMARK
COPENHAGEN 45 86841200
JUTLAND 86-84-12-00
DOMINICAN REPUBLIC
SANTIAGO 583-0351
SANTO DOMINGO 687-4943
ECUADOR
BABAHOYO 4-753-340
GUAYAQUIL 524-003
CUENCA 825-081
GUAYAQUIL 366-956
MANTA 612-405
QUITO 543-692
RIOBAMBA 964-619
EL SALVADOR
SAN SALVADOR 25-1430
CUSCATANCINGO 25-3064
SAN SALVADOR 21-1572
SANTA ANA 41-1006
FAROE ISLANDS
TORSHAVN 29810551
FINLAND
HELSINKI 90-71-20-58
HELSINKI 90-148-27-25
TAMPERE 931-55-14-00
FRANCE
ANGERS 41-8-49-48
ARRADON 97-44-76-76
ARGENTEUIL 34-10-04-20
AUXERRE 86-52-94-73
BREST 98-46-44-56
CORBEI 60-89-07-82
DUNKERQUE 28-66-16-96
LIMOGES 55-38-43-22
MACON 85-38-26-64
MARSEILLE 92-34-31-36
MELUN 64-09-40-02
METZ 87-50-70-73
NANTES 40-37-91-91
NICE 93-44-39-29
PARIS 43-25-75-00
PAYS DE GEX 50-42-56-28
QUIMPER 98-53-75-04
RENNES 99-87-01-20

ROUSSILLON 33-9005-7044
SAINT BRIEVC 96-62-31-06
SAINT DIE 29-56-76-66
ST. ETTIENNE 77-79-74-11
ST. GENIS POUILLY 50-42-26-28
SOTTEVTLE ROUEN 35-72-33-44
STRASBOURG 88-44-16-66
SURESNES 40-99-98-70
TOURCOING 20-24-08-75
VERSAILLES 39-50-72-62
VILLEURBANNE 78-85-53-88
GERMANY
AACHEN 241-19295
ANSBACH 981-19295
ASCHAFFENBURG 6021-74255
AUGSBURG 821-19295
BIELEFELD 521-19295
BOIZENBURG 38847-2954
BONN 228-19294
BREMEN 421-19295
BREMERHAVEN 471-58765
DELMENHORST 4221-53355
DORTMUND 231-19295
DUSSELDORF 211-19295
ERLANGEN 9131-19295
ESSEN 201-13295
FRANKFURT 69-19295
GELSENKIRCHEN 209-19295
GIESSEN 641-19295
HAGEN 2331-19295
HAMBURG 40-19295
HANNOVER 511-19295
HEILBRONN 7131-19295
KAISERSLAUTERN 631-19295
KARLSRUHE 721-19295
KOBLENZ 261-36830
KOLN 221-19295
LUDWIGSBURG 7141-19295
MANNHEIM 621-19295
MINDEN 571-21962
MUNICH (GSO) 89-3169500
MUNICH 89-19295
NURNBERG 911-19295
OBERHAUSEN 208-19295
OBERUSEL 494-6171-51270
OLDENBURG 441-19295
OSNABRUCK 541-23912
RHEINE 5971-19295
STUTTGART 711-19295
WUPPERTAL-BARMEN 202-19295
WURZBURG 931-883131
GUATEMALA
GUATEMALA 530065
HONDURAS
TEGUCIGALPA 504-226674
HUNGARY
BUDAPEST 361 136-2680
ICELAND
REYKJAVIK 354-5512010

The above numbers are NOT English-speaking.

INTERGROUP PHONE NUMBERS

VESTMANNAEYJAR	354-4811140
ISAFJORDUR	354-4563411
AKUREYRI	354-4622373
SELFOSS	354-4821787
EGILSSTADIR	354-4711972
KEFLAVIK	354-4211800
HAFNARFJORDUR	354-5658353
AKRANES	354-4312540

INDIA

BANGALORE	812-2215253
BOMBAY	22-5392951
CALCUTTA	33-492220
CHANDIGARH	172 565870
MADRAS	44-615300
NAGPUR	91-1536403
NEW DELHI	11-650802
PUNE	647265

ITALY

ROME	06-66-36-629
FIRENZE	0556503054
FLORENCE	055-6503254
PALERMO	091-6825903
PORDENONE	0434-521393
TORINO	011-4364978
VERONA	45-561587

JAPAN

TOKYO	03-3590-5377
HIROSHIMA	082-2959750
KAGOSHIMA CITY	0992-48-0057
NAGASAKI-SHI	0958-26-5343
NAGOYA	0529151602
OSAKA	6-5360828
SENDAI	022-2765210

LATVIA

RIGA	371 2-333523
YELGAVA	40120

LITHUANIA

VILNIUS	370 2-260017

LUXEMBOURG

LUXEMBOURG CITY	480322

MALTA

VALLETTA	356 335786

MEXICO

MEXICO CITY	5-12-0317
ACAPULCO	3-73-82
AGUASCALIENTES	574-97
ATEPEHUACAN	368-3943
CAMPECHE	981-609950
COLIMA	331-33730
CORODOBA	2-84-44
CUAUTLA	2-91-16
CUERNAVACA	73-143698
DURANGO	2-07-99
ECATEPEC	7-80-67-82
ECATEPEC DE MORELOS	7-87-28-36
FRESNILLO	23461
GOMEZ PALACIO	14 75 23
GUADALAJARA	3-6176472
GUZMAN	24300
GUAYMAS	622-28555
HIDALGO	40567
HUATUSCO	4-15-55
IGUALA	2-39-40
IRAPUATO	6-44-22
JALAPAA	28-179464
JOJUTLA	734-23125
JUAREZ	14-36-69
LA PEIDAD	2-51-79
LAGOS DE MORENO	2-11-99
LAZARO CARDENAS	2-19-10
LEON	7-61-47
LOS REYES	2-11-51
MERIDA	23-01-65
MEXICO CITY	3-68-39-43
MONTERREY	8-375-48-40
MORELIA	2-44-88
NAVOJOA	2-59-53
OBREGON	64-2-418-86
OCOTIAN	2-12-35
ORIZABA	27-25-69-77
PACHUCA	771-51971
PATZCUARO	2-02-55
POZA RICA	2-76-02
PUERTO VALLARTA	2-18-78
QUERETARO	6-87-77
SALAMANCA	8-35-99
SALTILLO	2-95-56
SAN CRISTOBAL	8-44-50
SAN LUIS POTOSI	48-18-07-01
SAN MARTIN	429-79
TAMPICO	2-56-34
TAPACHULA	625-37
TAXCO	2-29-36
TEPIC	2-61-30
TIJUANA	85-58-80
TLAQUEPAQUE	39-64-24
TOLUCA	72-258-24
TORREON	12-07-90
TUXTLA GUTIERREZ	2-35-86
URUAPAN	3-25-02
VALLE SANTIAGO	3-13-60
VERACRUZ	29-32-58-80
VILLAHERMOSA	4-03-18
ZACAPU	3-08-31
ZAPOPAN	6-33-18-39

NETHERLANDS

AMSTERDAM	020149481
DRIEBERGEN	03438-13102
HERTOGENBOSCH	073417553

NEVIS

CHARLESTOWN	8684695776

NICARAGUA

MANAGUA	662022
MASAYA	052-2693

NORWAY

OSLO	22-46-89-65
OSLO	222-08767
BERGEN	94 68 05 97
DRAMMEN	90 92 15 93
GJOVIK	92 64 84 52
KRISTIANSAND	042-70737
MJONDALEN	094-77168
RIDABU	030-60528
SARPSBORG	94 28 95 83
STAVANGER	04 536895
TRONDHEIM	73 53 18 38

PANAMA

AGUADULCE	976660
CHITRE	961225
DAVID	742316
PANAMA CITY	507 648962

PARAGUAY

ASUNCION	21-207896

PERU

CHIMBOTE	326031
CUSCO	226260
LIMA	429412
PALERMO	0440234140
TRUJILLO	44-247914

POLAND

KONIN (GSO)	63-624763
BOLESLAWIEC	795-3201
ELBAG	51-325689
KONIN	63-423384
OSTROW WIELKOPOLSKI	64-381164
RZESZOW	17-30539
SIEDLCE	25-435843
WARSAWA	22-6287526

PORTUGAL

LISBON	1-7162969

RUSSIA

MOSCOW	95-3509011
ST.PETERSBURG	7812-18111

SPAIN

AVILES	98-5511691
BARCELONA	93-3177777
BILBAO	4-4680575
CADIZ	56-897401
IRUN	94-3619338
LOGRONO	4-125-1339
MADRID	91-3418282
MARBELLA	95-2218211
MURCIA	968-268026
PALMA DE MALLORC	971-462586
PAMPLONA	948242444
PUERTO LUZ	928202638
SANTA CRUZ DE TENER	22-249498
SANTANDER	942-361066
SEVILLA	954-572661
SEVILLA	5-4572661
VALENCIA	963-317160
PONTEVEDRA	986-231122
VALENCIA	96-3917160
VIGO	86-430528
VITORIA	945-250417
ZARAGOZA	976-293835

SRI LANKA

NUGEGODA	1-511884

SWEDEN

HORBY	8-04151368
KALIX	911-16393
MALMOE	46-40-85750
MALUNG	280-12411
MORA	0250-16460
OSTERSUND	063-806-54
SOLLEFTEA	620-165592
STENUNGSSUND	031-184994
STOCKHOLM(GSO)	8-6422609
STOCKHOLM	08-7203843
UPSALA	46-18-55-688

SWITZERLAND

GENEVA	022-443322
ZURICH	01-370 13 8.

TAIWAN

KAOHSIUNG	226-5218
TAIPEI	8366994

TRINIDAD AND TOBAGO

CHAGAUNAS	(868)665-1.

URUGUAY

MONTEVIDEO	957241

VENEZUELA

BARQUISIMETO	05126620
CARACAS	27526914
MARACAIBO	061-233052
SAN CRISTOBAL	076444172

The above numbers are NOT English-speaking.

ORDER FORM - MINIMUM ORDER $10

Quantities cannot be combined for discount. All prices are US$. **Non-USA** orders by credit card only. These books are **not** available for sale to Canadian addresses. Same prices outside USA. Prices include regular shipping

Choose a shipping method:

- [ ] Basic Shipping 2-4 weeks
- [ ] Add 20% for Priority Mail

Qty.	Mini Edition	Workbook Edition	First Edition	Original Manuscript	Anonymous Press Index	Study Edition Burgundy	Study Edition Black/Gold	Study Edition Black/Silver
1	$2.25	$4.75	$15.00	$7.00	$1.00	$14.75		
10	$22	$43	$136	$64	$8	$119		
20	$40	$80	$245	$119	$14	$230		
50	$80	$190	$525	$280	$30	$500		
100	$135	$350	$920	$518	$50	$890		
500	$400	$1700						
1,000	$700	$3250						
10,000	$6500							

↑ If needed indicate quantity in **boxes**

To Order:

Write: The Anonymous Press • POBox 1212 • Malo WA 99150
Or call: 800)800-4398 • (914)962-0708 • Fax (914)962-1395
UK 0800-96-2375• Australia 800-112-685• Eire 800-55-7896

Choose a payment method:

- [ ] Check, USA only, payable to: The Anonymous Press
- [ ] VISA/Mastercard Card number | | | | | | | | | | | | | | | | } Exp. date ___/___

Name _____

Street _____

City, State _____ Zip _____

Signature _____

ORDER FORM - MINIMUM ORDER $10

Quantities cannot be combined for discount. All prices are US$. **Non-USA** orders by credit card only. These books are **not** available for sale to Canadian addresses. Same prices outside USA. Prices include regular shipping

Choose a shipping method:

☐ Basic Shipping 2-4 weeks   ☐ Add 20% for Priority Mail

If needed indicate quantity in boxes

Qty.	Mini Edition	Workbook Edition	First Edition	Original Manuscript	Anonymous Press Index	Study Edition Burgundy	Study Edition Black/Gold	Study Edition Black/Silver
1	$2.25	$4.75	$15.00	$7.00	$1.00	$14.75		
10	$22	$43	$136	$64	$8	$119		
20	$40	$80	$245	$119	$14	$230		
50	$80	$190	$525	$280	$30	$500		
100	$135	$350	$920	$518	$50	$890		
500	$400	$1700						
1,000	$700	$3250						
10,000	$6500							

To Order:

Write: The Anonymous Press • PO Box 1212 • Malo WA 99150
Or call: (800)800-4398 • (914)962-0708 • Fax (914)962-1395
UK 0800-96-2375 • Australia 800-112-685 • Eire 800-55-7896

Choose a payment method:

☐ Check, USA only, payable to: The Anonymous Press

☐ VISA/Mastercard Card number ⟩ Exp. date _____ / ____

Name _____

Street _____

City, State _____ Zip _____

Signature _____

Phone (_____

ISBN 0-9637666-0-0